Making Movies on Your PC

DREAM UP, DESIGN, AND DIRECT 3-D MOVIES

David Mason
Alexander Enzmann

Waite Group Press™
Corte Madera, California

Publisher: *Mitchell Waite*
Editorial Director: *Scott Calamar*
Managing Editor: *John Crudo*
Content Editor: *Heidi Brumbaugh*
Technical Reviewer: *Bruce Goren and John Blanchard*
Design: *Cecile Kaufman and Pat Rogondino*
Production: *Jimmie Young*
Illustrations: *Ben Long*
Cover Design: *Michael Rogondino*
Production Director: *Julianne Ososke*

Printed in the United States of America
9394 9596 •10 98 7 6 5 4 3 2 1

Library of Congress Cataloging in Publication Data
ISBN: 1-878739-41-7: $34.95
Mason, David (David Keith), 1964—
    Making movies on your PC : dream up, design, and direct 3-D movies
  / David Mason, Alexander Enzmann.
      p. cm.
    Includes index.
    ISBN 1-878739-41-7
    1. Computer animation. 2. Computer graphics. I. Enzmann, Alexander. II. Title.
TR897.5.M37 1993
006.6'865—dc20   93-3388
                                CIP

DEDICATION

This book is for Wendy.
(Alexander Enzmann)

To Mom.
(David Mason)

ACKNOWLEDGMENTS

The authors give their thanks to Mitchell Waite for thinking this book up and for giving us the opportunity to write it; to Dan Farmer, for pointing Mitch in our direction; to John Crudo, for managing everything so well; to Heidi Brumbaugh for her great editing job; to Bruce Goren, whose technical review kept us from putting our feet in our mouths; to Julianne Ososke and the rest of the Production crew; to Jeff Bowermaster, Will Wagner, and the Trilobyte folks for their contributions; to the owners of the Cafe Pamplona, a great place to swill coffee and discuss animation; and to Marilyn Mason for her help with printing, mailing, reading, and numerous other tasks.

ABOUT THE AUTHORS

ALEXANDER ENZMANN

Alexander Enzmann first became interested in ray tracing after David K. Mason introduced him to the QRT and DKB raytracers. From early efforts with DKB, Alexander continued on to join the Persistence of Vision team in the development of the POV-Ray raytracer. As an exercise in modeling and graphics code, he developed the Polyray raytracer. Formerly a nationally ranked pairs figure skater, he and his wife still find some time once in a while for death spirals and lifts. Alexander has BA and MS degrees in Mathematics from the University of Massachusetts and Northeastern University. He has worked in computer security and undersea surveillance. At the present, he provides systems and requirements analysis for aircraft mission planning. He is currently a Member of the Technical Staff at The MITRE Corporation in Bedford, Massachusetts.

DAVID K. MASON

Dave Mason became obsessed with computer graphics (of a sort) as a teenager, fiddling away on a black and white TRS-80 Model I. Now an after-hours 3-D rendering and animation freak, he's the author of DTA, DMorf, and a few other computer animation utilities. In real life, he works at a major software house, writing programs which, alas, have absolutely nothing whatsoever to do with making movies. He received a degree in English at Northeastern University.

PREFACE

This book and the accompanying disks are an introduction to 3-D computer graphics animation. This book focuses on how to make sequences of 3-D graphic images, assemble them into an animation file, and then display the animation. Several tools are provided: Polyray, DTA, PLAY, SP, and DMorf. Through the course of this book you will be introduced to these tools and how they can be used to create short movies.

What's in the Book

- Chapter 1, *Introduction*, gives an overview of what makes up a 3-D animation. The process of building an animation is described, together with an introduction to the tools that are used for each step.

- Chapter 2, *Getting Your Feet Wet*, takes you on a quick trip through the process of generating the frames of an animation with Polyray, producing an animation with DTA, then playing the animation with Play.

- Chapter 3, *Making a Movie in Eight Steps*, is a more detailed tutorial. It goes into the details of building a Polyray animation data file from scratch.

- Chapter 4, *Advanced Techniques*, provides tips and techniques for building animations. Covered topics include moving objects along paths, animating textures, and animating lights.

■◀ **Chapter 5,** *Movie-Making Tools*, goes into depth on the capabilities and features of each of the tools included with the book.

■◀ **Chapter 6,** *The Movie Pages*, presents several completed animations. This chapter gives an explanation of what each one does and how it was built. The data files for all of these animations are on the included disk.

■◀ **Appendix A,** *References*, tells you where to go to find more information about rendering and computer animation.

■◀ **Appendix B,** *The Movie Contest*, explains the details of the *Making Movies on the PC* animation contest.

Shareware

Most of the programs included with this book (Polyray, DMorf, Play, and DTA) are distributed as shareware. Shareware is a way to evaluate software on a trial basis to make sure it performs the functions you need. If you continue to use the programs beyond the trial period, you are obligated to register the programs with their authors. Specific rules and restrictions can be found in the documentation for the individual programs.

Support for these programs is available directly from the authors. All of them provide support on CompuServe. Polyray, DTA, and DMorf are supported in the GRAPHDEV forum (GO GRAPHDEV). Play is supported in the ASOFT forum (GO ASOFT). You can also write to the authors at the addresses provided in the documentation accompanying each program.

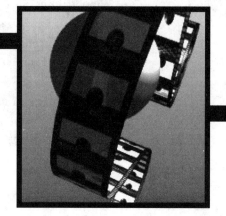

TABLE OF CONTENTS

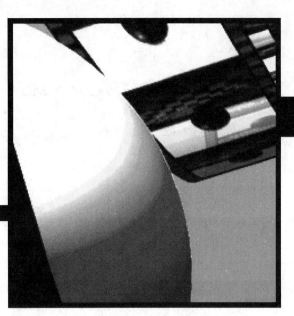

CONTENTS

Chapter 1: Introduction 1

Chapter 2: Getting Your Feet Wet 11

Chapter 3: Making A Movie in Eight Steps 17

Chapter 4: Advanced Techniques 35

Chapter 5: Movie-Making Tools 75

Chapter 6: The Movie Pages   165

1 INTRODUCTION

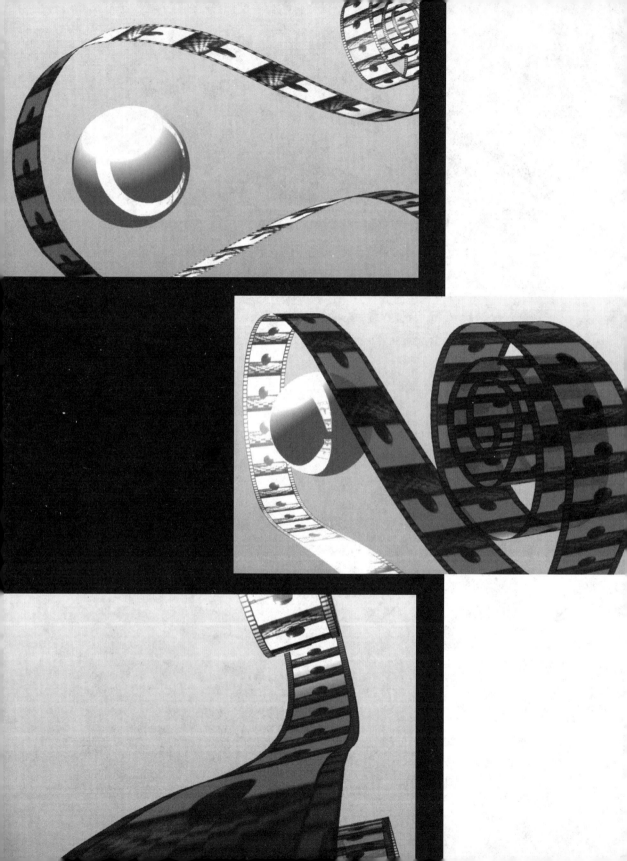

1 INTRODUCTION

Welcome to the world of 3-D computer graphics animation. This book will describe the basic tools and techniques needed to generate short animations on your PC. The type of animation we will work with is not the traditional cel animation used for decades in the motion picture industry, but a form of animation in which you model and view, using computer programs and data, objects moving around in a three-dimensional virtual world.

Several tools are provided: Polyray, DTA, PLAY, DMorf, and SP. Through the course of this book, you will be introduced to these tools and how they can be used to create short movies.

HOW THE PROS DO IT

Professional animation is usually the result of talented artists using expensive tools. At the top tier, animation companies like Pixar and Rhythm & Hues employ high-end specialized (read that expensive) hardware, proprietary software, teams of artists and programmers, and budgets that real human beings can only imagine. A second level of professional animators uses off-the-shelf software solutions. Some of these run on high-end hardware like the Iris Indigo, and others work on a souped-up PC or Macintosh. In the PC world, the king is Autodesk's 3D Studio. 3D Studio does it all, but with a price tag in the thousands of dollars, it's beyond the reach of the amateur or casual animator. Some new solutions, like 3D Workshop (Brown-Wagh) and Will Vinton's Playmation (Hash Enterprises), are beginning to approach affordability, but they are still expensive for a hobby.

THE HACKER'S ALTERNATIVE

If you don't have $3,000 to spend on software alone, but still want to create computer animation, you're not alone. A number of part-time graphics freaks, either fed up with the prices or unavailability of commercial rendering and animation tools, or just stuck with a bit too much free time, built their own. Congregating on computer bulletin board systems and online services, these graphics hackers learn from each other, swap home-grown tools, and create amazing pictures and animations. Their achievements include such rendering programs as DKB-Trace, POV-Ray, Vivid, and Polyray; modeling tools like VVFONT, CTDS, and Worm; animation tools like Play, DTA, and Animake; image processing tools like PICLAB, Improcess, and DMorf; and fractal programs like FRACTINT and WinFRACT.

On the companion disk to this book, we have included a package of some of these tools, which work well together. Using these tools, you won't get an integrated environment or good visual modeling. What you will get is the ability to make slick-looking stuff if you're willing to put in some time and play a lot.

CONCEPTS AND TERMINOLOGY

Before you move on to the rest of this book, here are some of the basic concepts you're going to need to understand, and some buzzwords you'll need to recognize for the rest of this book to make sense.

THE 3-D COORDINATE SYSTEM

Any location in the virtual worlds that you create can be described with a 3-D coordinate, a set of three floating-point numbers that represent the location's distance from the center (or origin) of the universe along three axes: x, y, and z. The x-axis is usually used for the left-to-right dimension. A negative x value means that a coordinate is located to the left of the world origin, while a positive x value means it's on the right. y is used to represent up-and-down (negative is down, positive is up). The z-axis moves forward-to-backward (negative is forward, positive is backward). The origin would be coded "<0,0,0>," and a point one unit to the right would be "<1,0,0>." In Figure 1-1, you can see how a 3-D point that is labeled <-1,3,-4> would be placed. It is one unit to the left of the origin along the x-axis, three units above the origin along the y-axis, and four units in front of the origin along the z-axis.

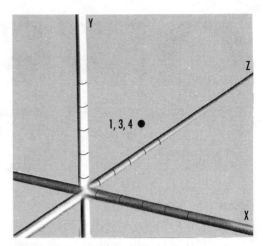

Figure 1-1 A 3-D Point

The numbers you use for 3-D coordinates don't necessarily have any meaning in the real world. One unit could represent a million miles, or it could represent half an inch. You decide the scale.

OBJECTS

The basic geometric shapes (such as the sphere, box, cone, disk, and triangle) and some not-so-basic shapes (like the torus or donut, polynomial, height field, Bezier patch, and triangular patch) are called primitives. They're called

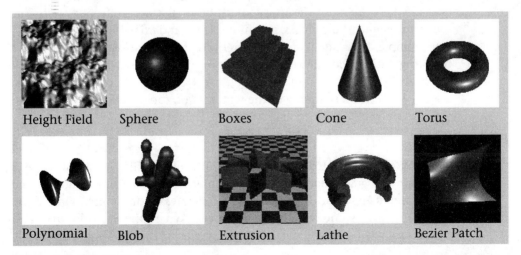

Height Field   Sphere   Boxes   Cone   Torus

Polynomial   Blob   Extrusion   Lathe   Bezier Patch

Figure 1-2 Primitives

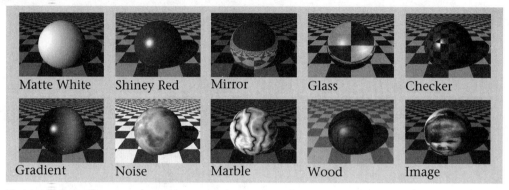

Figure 1-3 Textures

that because these shapes can be used as building blocks to produce other, more complicated shapes. Figure 1-2 shows a sampling of the types of objects you can create with Polyray.

You can use a technique called *Constructive Solid Geometry,* or *CSG,* to carve shapes apart or stick them together. An object can be a single primitive, or it can be multiple primitives combined with CSG. The process of designing and creating objects is called modeling.

TEXTURES

In addition to controlling the shapes of objects, you can control how their surfaces look. You can specify such attributes as color, reflection, transparency, turbulence, bumpiness, and more. The standard, white marble texture, for example, has a small amount of reflectivity, no transparency, and white coloring with turbulent veins of black running through it. By combining such attributes in different ways, you can create a wide range of textures. Figure 1-3 shows a sampling of the textures you can produce with Polyray.

RENDERING

When you have created a virtual world, it's time to film it. A renderer is a computer program that works like a camera. It reads a description of the scene and, using a lot of mathematics, generates color pictures. One of the objects in your scene will always be an eye. Where the eye is located, and what it's pointing at, will determine what ends up on the computer screen.

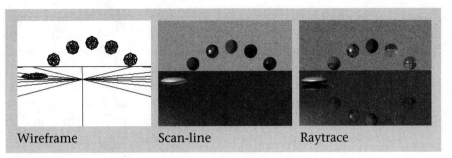

| Wireframe | Scan-line | Raytrace |

Figure 1-4 Rendering Methods

Polyray, the rendering program included with this book, can handle three different rendering methods. In wireframe rendering, the computer draws lines representing the outline and internal structure of the objects. In scan-line rendering, the objects are filled in and shaded. In raytracing, the computer simulates the operation of light-rays to shade the objects. Use raytracing to represent such optical effects as shadows, reflection, and refraction. A wireframe render is usually very quick; scan-line is not as quick. Raytracing usually takes much longer than the other methods. Figure 1-4 shows the kind of output you can expect from each of the rendering methods.

ANIMATION

Computer animation is based on the same principle as traditional animation: display a lot of pictures, one after the other, real fast. If the pictures are moving fast enough, the viewer's eye will be fooled into seeing movement. Each separate picture in an animation is called a *frame*.

There are a number of terms used interchangeably to refer to animated scenes. In addition to "movie" and "animation," we sometimes refer to them as *flics*. A flic is an animation file in the .FLI (or .FLC) file format. This type of file first appeared in Autodesk's Animator program, but now it's everywhere.

A *looping* animation is one where the final frame is the same as the first, so there's no break or skip if it's displayed repeatedly. For example, in a looping flic, you might see a ball bounce up in the air and fall back down to where it started. When you play it continuously, you get a ball that just keeps bouncing forever. In a nonlooping animation, the ball might bounce up into the air and stop. When you play it continuously, it appears to bounce up, then mysteriously disappear and reappear on the ground again. Because most of the flics you create will be relatively short, looping is important. Constant jumping and skipping can be extremely annoying to the viewer.

Morphing is shorthand for metamorphosis, or making one object turn smoothly into another. There are two ways to do morphing. The most common, as seen in such movies as *Willow* and *Star Trek VI*, and in tons of television commercials, is an image processing technique, in which a two-dimensional picture is warped and faded into another. The other morphing method is to warp a three-dimensional model of one object into another shape.

TOOLS ON THE DISK

This book includes both Freeware and Shareware programs that assist in the generation of animations. The programs include

- Polyray—A rendering program that reads ASCII data and generates rendered images in Targa format.
- DTA—A versatile image format conversion program. We will use it for assembling a sequence of frames into a flic file.
- PLAY—This program plays a flic file on your VGA or SVGA.
- SP—Generates weird, 3-D spline-curve paths for objects.
- DMorf—A 2-D image morphing program.

These tools, plus an ASCII text editor, are enough to produce excellent short animation. The quality of the animations you can create using these tools is limited only by your imagination, computer speed, and patience. As you work through the book, you will be introduced to each of the component programs and how they are used. This book is only a starting point — there are more documents specific to the tools on the included disks.

HARDWARE REQUIREMENTS

To use the software included with this book, you must have an MS-DOS computer with an 80286 or better processor, a VGA monitor, and at least two megabytes of memory. We strongly recommend at least an 80386 processor, a math coprocessor chip, and as much disk space and memory as you can obtain by legal means.

A low-resolution, 30-frame version of the "Bouncing Ball" movie required over five hours to render on a 16-Mhz 80286 computer with an 80287 math coprocessor. It rendered in just 22 minutes on a 33-Mhz 80486. On a 50-Mhz 80486, it only took 16 minutes.

SOFTWARE INSTALLATION

To install the movie-making tools, insert the disk labeled "Tools" in your 5¼ inch floppy disk drive. If you have a '386- or '486-based computer, type

```
C:\> a:tinstall a: c:
```

If your machine has a '286 chip in it, type

```
C:\> a:tinst286 a: c:
```

Wait! If your 5¼-inch drive is drive B, then use "b:" instead of "a:." If you want these files installed on a drive other than drive C, then use that drive letter instead of "c:."

When the batch installation program is done, the movie-making tools will be in a directory called \MOVIES\TOOLS, and their document files will be located in \MOVIES\DOCS\.

To install the demonstration files from the various chapters of this book, insert the disk labeled "demonstration files" and type

```
C:\> a:sinstall a: c:
```

When that's done, the files for this chapter (if there were any, which there aren't) would be in \MOVIES\CHAP1. The files for Chapter 2, *Getting Your Feet Wet,* are in \MOVIES\CHAP2, and so on.

2 GETTING YOUR FEET WET

2 GETTING YOUR FEET WET

In this chapter, we go through the steps required to create a simple movie. We'll use the three main tools provided with this book: Polyray, to render the individual frames of the animation; DTA, to combine these frames into a flic; and Play, to display the results on your screen.

The first step is to build a data file that describes all of the objects and textures and movements. That gets complicated, so we'll skip it for now and use a pre-built data file, LOGO.PI.

First, change to the directory on your hard disk that contains the sample files for this chapter:

```
C:\> cd \movies\chap2
```

Take a quick look at LOGO.PI, shown in Listing 2-1. You can use the DOS EDIT command to view these text files. You'll see that it's a regular text file:

LISTING 2.1 LOGO.PI

```
// animation settings
total_frames 30
start_frame 0
end_frame 29
outfile logo
define rotation ((frame/total_frames)*360)

// set up camera
viewpoint {
 from <0,0,-12>
 at <0,0,0>
 up <0,1,0>
 angle 45
 hither 1
 resolution 160,100
```

```
  aspect 1.333333
}

// library files
include "colors.inc"
include "letters.inc"

// include a sky and a lightsource
background Pink
light <-10, 10, -10>

// place the letters for the word "Making"
object {
 capital_m
 + lowercase_a { translate <1.7,0,0 > }
 + lowercase_k { translate <3.15,0,0 > }
 + lowercase_i { translate <3.85,0,0 > }
 + lowercase_n { translate <4.85,0,0 > }
 + lowercase_g { translate <6.25,0,0 > }
 shiny_blue
 translate <-3,1.3,0>
 rotate <0,-rotation,0>
}

// place the letters for the word "Movies"
object {
 capital_m
 + lowercase_o { translate <1.7,0,0 > }
 + lowercase_v { translate <3,0,0 > }
 + lowercase_i { translate <3.925,0,0 > }
 + lowercase_e { translate <4.875,0,0 > }
 + lowercase_s { translate <6.2,0,0 > }
 shiny_blue
 translate <-3,-1.3,0>
 rotate <0,rotation,0>
}
```

For now, don't worry about what all that means. We'll get to those kinds
of details soon enough. For a discussion of this data file, refer to Chapter 6,
The Movie Pages.

> For best results, make sure that the subdirectory with the utilities
> `C:\MOVIES\TOOLS`
> was added to the AUTOEXEC.BAT file before starting up your system.

RUN POLYRAY

To run Polyray on our sample file, type

```
C:\MOVIES\CHAP2> polyray logo.pi -r1 -V1
```

> Make sure to type commands just as they appear in the text; Polyray is case-sensitive!

As Polyray starts drawing pictures, numbers generate on your screen as your system computes the animation instruction. Figure 2-1 shows what the final animation sequence ought to look like. Once computed Polyray saves the pictures on your disk as LOGO001.TGA, LOGO002.TGA, LOGO003.TGA, all the way on up to LOGO029.TGA.

RUN DTA

Assemble all the TGA files into a flic by typing

```
C:\MOVIES\CHAP2> dta logo*.tga /ologo /s5
```

DTA creates a flic file called LOGO.FLI.
The /O switch determines the name of the new flic file. If you don't specify a name with the /O switch, the default file name is ANIM.FLI.

PLAY THE FLIC

Run the Trilobyte PLAY program on the flic:

```
C:\MOVIES\CHAP2> play logo.fli
```

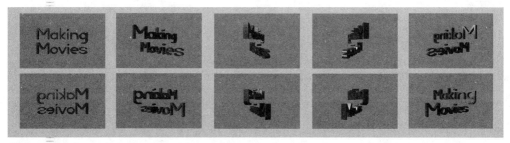

Figure 2-1 The LOGO Animation

And that's all there is to it. Sit back and enjoy it. If the animation appears to be too fast or slow, you can adjust it by pressing a number key. When you get bored, press the (ESC) key to exit PLAY.

CLEAN UP AFTER YOURSELF

You probably won't need these .TGA files any more, so get rid of them:

```
C:\MOVIES\CHAP2> del logo*.tga
```

3 MAKING A MOVIE IN EIGHT STEPS

3 MAKING A MOVIE IN EIGHT STEPS

There are many ways to create a 3-D animation, probably as many ways as there are animators. Some folks prefer to map everything out beforehand on graph paper, some like to wade right in with no preconceptions. Regardless of your approach, you must build a data file describing objects and how they move. In this chapter, we present one way to build a small movie from scratch.

STEP 1: THINK IT OUT

There's no law that says you can't just wade right in and start writing your data file, but you could save yourself a lot of effort and grief later on if you stop and think things through now. Before you get down to business, you should build up at least a vague idea of what you want your movie to be like. Ask yourself the following questions: What objects are in the scene? Where are they placed? Which objects move, and how? What's in the background?

Get away from your computer, drink some coffee, and doodle on napkins. Experience has shown that the Cafe Pamplona, near Harvard Square in Cambridge, Massachusetts, is the best place to do this (but any Dunkin Donuts should serve almost as well).

For our first project, let's start simple. Let's try three spheres rolling around on a traditional red-and-green checkered plane. It would be rather boring for all three to travel along identical paths, so we'll make them move independently. The first two can roll around in circles in opposite directions. The paths should intersect, but the spheres should never touch. The last sphere can travel in a larger circle around the others. Because this one has farther to go, we'll make it move slower than the others. Figure 3-1 shows an overhead view.

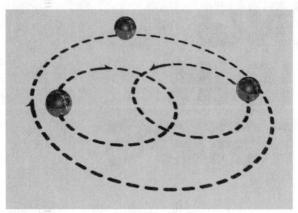

Figure 3-1 Overhead View of spheres rolling on a plane

These objects and paths will need dimensions. Make each of the spheres 1 unit in size. The large circular path is a 10-unit circle, centered on the origin. The left circular path is a 4-unit circle, centered on <3,0,0>, and the right circular path is another 4-unit circle, centered on <-3,0,0>.

STEP 2: CREATE A DATA FILE

Now we can get down to the business of building a Polyray data file based on our little idea. So, open up a new text file, called ROLLERS.PI, with your text editor and we will get started. Before we can begin to define our spheres, we will need some standard header information as shown in Listing 3-1:

LISTING 3-1 ROLLERS.PI

```
total_frames 100
start_frame 0
end_frame 99
outfile rolb

viewpoint {
  from <0,5,-23>
  at <0,0,0>
  up <0,1,0>
  angle 45
```

```
    hither 1
    resolution 160,100
    aspect 1.333333
    }

include "colors.inc"
include "texture.inc"
light <-10, 10, -10>

object {
 disc <0,-1,0>,<0,1,0>,0,1000
 texture { checker shiny_red, shiny_blue }
}

object {
 sphere <0,0,4>,1
 rotate <0,((frame/total_frames)*720)+180,0>
 steel_blue
 translate <-3,0,0>
}

object {
 sphere <0,0,4>,1
 rotate <0,-(frame/total_frames)*720,0>
 steel_blue
 translate <3,0,0>
}

object {
 sphere <0,0,10>,1
 rotate <0,-(frame/total_frames)*360,0>
 steel_blue
}
```

The include statements make standard color and texture definitions, such as shiny_red and white_marble, available to the data file. The viewpoint describes the virtual camera that takes the picture. The from statement defines the location of the camera, at defines where it's looking, up decides which directions are up and down, and angle defines the camera's aperture. The resolution statement defines the dimensions of the picture and aspect

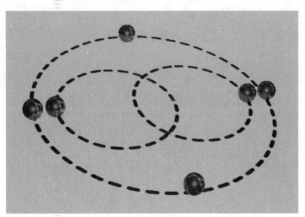

Figure 3-2 Placeholders

defines the ratio of height to width. The aspect ratio is set to 1.333 because in 320x200 mode, with its non-square pixels, 160 horizontal pixels are approximately 1.333 times wider than 100 vertical pixels. If the pixels were square, we would have to set the aspect ratio to 1.6 instead. The light statement installs a light source, so our objects will not be moving around in the dark.

If we decide that the larger circular path has a radius of 9 units and is centered on the world origin (coordinate <0,0,0>), and that the smaller paths have radii of 4 units and are centered on coordinates <-3,0,0> and <3,0,0> respectively, we can define some placeholder spheres:

```
object { sphere <-7,0,0>,1 }
object { sphere <7,0,0>,1 }
object { sphere <0,0,10>,1 }
object { sphere <0,0,-10>,1 }
object { sphere <10,0,0>,1 }
object { sphere <-10,0,0>,1 }
```

The first two spheres each lie on one of the small circular paths. The rest lie on the maximum and minimum x- and z-coordinates for the larger path. From above, the scene ought to look something like Figure 3-2. We'll use these spheres to test camera placement.

The marbles also need some ground to roll around on, but let's save that until we're done with the rest of the scene. A floor takes much longer for Polyray to display than a few spheres, because it fills so much of the screen. Because you're going to be rendering this whole animation several times while we work on it, you'll want to save as much time as you can.

Figure 3-3 Poor Camera Placement

STEP 3: TEST RENDER

Run Polyray against the data file in fast scan-line mode. Remember, the command is case-sensitive.

```
C:\> MOVIES\CHAP3>rollers.pi -r1 -V 1
```

Polyray will render to the screen. As Figure 3-3 demonstrates, the camera location that we started with, <0,5,-10>, is too close. We can't see all of the objects in the scene.

Edit the data file and move the camera farther back, all the way out to <0,5,-25>. Run Polyray again to see if your new camera distance works. It does, as you can see in Figure 3-4.

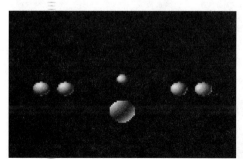

Figure 3-4 From a Better Camera Position

STEP 4: MAKE THEM MOVE

In order to generate an animation, we will have to make a change to the header information at the top of ROLLERS.PI. At the very top of the file, insert this frame-count information:

```
// Animation settings
outfile rolla
total_frames 10
start_frame 0
end_frame 9
```

These lines will tell Polyray to create ten pictures, starting with ROLL000.TGA and ending with ROLL009.TGA.

The next thing we need to do is figure out how to make a sphere move around in a circle. We could do this with a combination of the sine and cosine functions, but it's quicker and easier to use Polyray's Rotate command. Rotate transforms an object by turning it around the world origin (the <0,0,0> coordinate). If an object is located at the origin, then rotating it will just change the direction the object is pointing in, but if we move it away from the origin, the whole object will move in a circle around the origin. The radius of this circle will be defined by the distance between the origin and the center of the object. In Figure 3-5, a sphere at coordinate <5,0,0> rotates 90 degrees around the y-axis, and ends up at coordinate <0,0,-5>.

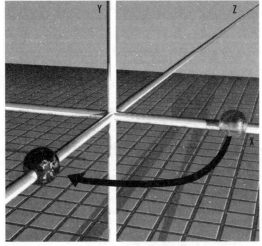

Figure 3-5 A sphere rotates 90° around the y-axis

Because we want the first sphere to move in a circle with a radius of 4, we need to place it 4 units away from the world origin:

```
// sphere 1
object {
  sphere <0,0,4>,1
}
```

To make the sphere rotate around the origin, we add a rotate command to the object definition:

```
object {
  sphere <0,0,4>,1
  rotate <0,5,0>
}
```

We've rotated the sphere into a new position, but it still is not moving. If we were to generate an animation right now, it would just sit there, rotated five degrees. We need to link the rotation to the animation frame counter:

```
object {
  sphere <0,0,4>,1
  rotate <0,frame,0>
}
```

Now the sphere moves. In the first frame (frame zero), the sphere is in its initial position. In frame 1, the sphere has rotated 1 degree. In frame 2, it has rotated 2 degrees, and so on. The problem with this solution is that at the end of this 10-frame animation, the sphere will have rotated only 10 degrees, and a full circle is 360 degrees. We would have to render 360 frames to get that sphere to move all the way around the circle. Fortunately, instead of just using the frame counter, we can use an equation containing the frame counter:

```
object {
  sphere <0,0,4>,1
  rotate <0,frame*36,0>
}
```

That causes the sphere to rotate 36 degrees for each frame, moving it all the way around the circle in the animation's 10 frames. Are we all set? Not quite. What if, later on, we want to make the animation longer, say to 60 frames? We could go back into the data file at that point and change the frame*36 to frame*6, because 6 x 60 = 360. But why should we have to do math every time we want to change the length of the animation? That's what computers are for! Polyray already knows how long the animation is, because at the top of the file we supplied a `total_frames` value. We can change the equation so that it uses `total_frames` as well as `frame`:

```
object {
  sphere <0,0,4>,1
  rotate <0,(frame/total_frames)*360,0>
}
```

Now the sphere will rotate exactly 360 degrees over the course of the animation, regardless of how many frames we're rendering.

This sphere now moves in a circle, but the center of the circle is <0,0,0>, and according to the diagram the center should be <-3,0,0>. Polyray's Translate command can fix this problem. Translate transforms an object by adding to or subtracting from its coordinates. Figure 3-6 shows how Polyray translates a sphere.

By adding a translate to the object definition, like this:

```
object {
  sphere <0,0,4>,1
  rotate <0,(frame/total_frames)*360,0>
  translate <-3,0,0>
}
```

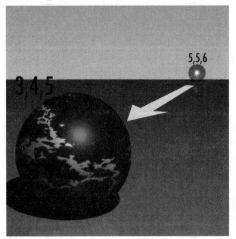

Figure 3-6 Translating an Object by <2,1,1>

you change the initial location of the sphere from <0,0,4> to <-3,0,4>, and you also change the center of the circle that it rotates around from <0,0,0> to <-3,0,0>. To complete the scene, just add two more sphere definitions:

```
// Sphere 2
object {
  sphere <0,0,4>,1
  rotate <0,-(frame/total_frames)*360,0>
  translate <3,0,0>
}

// Sphere 3
object {
  sphere <0,0,10>,1
  rotate <0,(frame/total_frames)*360,0>
}
```

The first travels in a 3-unit circle around coordinate <3,0,0> and the second travels in a 10-unit circle around coordinate <0,0,0>. If the edits have been made correctly to ROLLERS.PI, it now looks just like ROLL1.PI, which is in C:\MOVIES\CHAP3. Listing 3-2 shows the complete edited code.

LISTING 3-2 ROLL1.PI

```
// Animation settings
outfile rolla
total_frames 10
start_frame 0
end_frame 9

include "colors.inc"
include "texture.inc"

viewpoint {
  from <0,5,-25>
  at <0,0,0>
  up <0,1,0>
  angle 45
  hither 1
  resolution 160,100
  aspect 1.333
}

light <-10,10,-10>

// Sphere 1
object {
```

continued on next page

continued from previous page

```
    sphere <0,0,4>,1
    rotate <0,(frame/total_frames)*360,0>
    translate <-3,0,0>
}

// Sphere 2
object {
    sphere <0,0,4>,1
    rotate <0,-(frame/total_frames)*360,0>
    translate <3,0,0>
}

// Sphere 3
object {
    sphere <0,0,10>,1
    rotate <0,(frame/total_frames)*360,0>
}
```

STEP 5: TEST ANIMATE

Try the edited file.

Run Polyray against ROLLERS.PI again:

```
C:\MOVIES\CHAP3\> polyray rollers.pi -r1 -V 1
```

This time, because of the changes in the file header, Polyray will display the picture 10 times, creating output files called ROLL000.TGA, ROLL001.TGA, and so on up to ROLL009.TGA, as shown in Figure 3-7. Compile the Targa files into a flic file:

```
C:\MOVIES\CHAP3\> dta roll*.tga /orollers
```

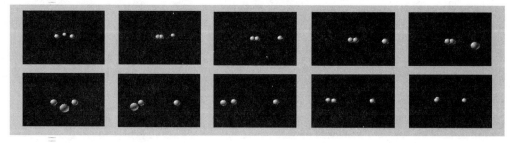

Figure 3-7 The Test Animation

28

The /O switch tells DTA to use the word "rollers" in the output file name, so DTA will generate a file called ROLLERS.FLI. Display the flic:

```
C:\MOVIES\CHAP3\> play rollers.fli
```

Slow the flic display down by pressing the number 5 on your keyboard.

STEP 6: FIX WHAT'S BROKEN

The flic looks okay, except for a few problems. First, the balls circling in the middle keep slamming into each other. That's because their paths are intersecting mirror images. We can keep them from passing through each other by making sure that one of the spheres gets to that intersection before the other. Just add 90 degrees to the rotation for the first sphere:

```
// sphere 1
object {
  sphere <0,0,4>,1
  rotate <0,90+((frame/total_frames)*360),0>
  translate <-3,0,0>
}
```

Another problem is that the sphere in the outside circle is moving too fast. It has farther to travel than the spheres on the inner circles, but it's being rotated at the same speed. We can't just slow it down, or it won't make a full circle by the end of the animation. You can, however, speed up the other two spheres for the same effect by causing them to travel two full, still rotations instead of one. Do this by multiplying the 360 degree arc by two:

```
rotate <0,90+((frame/total_frames)*(360*2)),0>
```

The data file at this point should look like Listing 3-3. You can also refer to ROLL2.PI, in C:\MOVIES\CHAP3, which includes the same edits.

LISTING 3-3 ROLL2.PI

```
// Rolling spheres

// animation settings
outfile rollb
total_frames 10
```

continued on next page

continued from previous page

```
start_frame 0
end_frame 9

// library files
include "colors.inc"
include "texture.inc"

viewpoint {
  // camera settings
  from <0,5,-25>
  at <0,0,0>
  up <0,1,0>
  angle 45
  hither 1
  // output file settings
  resolution 160,100
  aspect 1.333
}

// light source
light <-10,10,-10>

// sphere 1
object {
  sphere <0,0,4>,1
  rotate <0,90+(frame/total_frames)*(360*2),0>
  translate <-3,0,0>
}

// sphere 2
object {
  sphere <0,0,4>,1
  rotate <0,-(frame/total_frames)*(360*2),0>
  translate <3,0,0>
}
// sphere 3
object {
  sphere <0,0,10>,1
  rotate <0,(frame/total_frames)*360,0>
}
```

Render your edited file (ROLLERS.PI) again to make sure that these fixes did what you expected them to do. Follow the same steps you took in Step 5. Figure 3-8 illustrates the results.

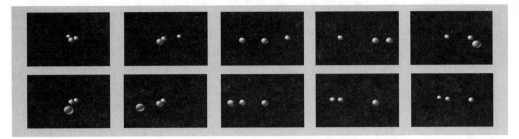

Figure 3-8 Testing the Fixes

STEP 7: FIDDLE WITH THE DATA FILE SOME MORE

If this flic looks good enough to you, skip ahead to Step 8. If it bores you, stick around for a while. We can try a few more things to liven it up some.

The spheres don't have to look as plain as they do. All Polyray objects have a texture. If you don't define one yourself, Polyray will just assign that rather boring matte-white texture. You can create a texture yourself, or use one of the predefined textures included in the TEXTURES.INC file, like `shiny_red` or `white_marble`. Because our spheres look sort of like marbles already, let's use `white_marble`:

```
// sphere 1
object {
  sphere <0,0,4>,1
  white_marble
  rotate <0,90+((frame/total_frames)*(360*2)),0>
  translate <-3,0,0>
}
```

The `white_marble` declaration goes before the `rotate` and `translate` transformations because we want the texture to move along with the marbles. If you re-render the flic and look closely at the spheres, you'll notice that there's still a problem with the texture. The spheres appear to be gliding, rather than rolling. Figure 3-9 illustrates this effect.

Figure 3-9 Gliding Marbles

To fix this you'll need to add one more `rotate` to each sphere, before the one that's already there. This will give it some spin:

```
// sphere 1
object {
 sphere <0,0,4>,1
 white_marble
 rotate <0,0,-((frame/total_frames)*(360*6))>
 rotate <0,90+((frame/total_frames)*(360*2)),0>
 translate <-3,0,0>
}
```

Because the sphere starts out right on the z-axis, rotating on z will turn the sphere around without moving it. The second rotation will move the rolling sphere around in a circle just like it did before.

Now would also be a good time to add that floor to the scene. Put a large checkerboard-patterned rectangle into the scene, at coordinate <0,-1,0>. It has to be placed 1 unit below the origin because the spheres reach that low.

When it's all done, the edited data file, which is also provided as ROLL4.PI, will look like Listing 3-4. Figure 3-10 illustrates this effect.

LISTING 3-4 ROLL4.PI

```
//animation settings
outfile rolld
total_frames 200
start_frame 0
end_frame 199

viewpoint {
   //camera settings
   from <0,5,-23>
   at <0,0,0>
   up <0,1,0>
   angle 45
   hither 1
   //output file settings
   resolution 320,200
   aspect 1.333333
   }

//library files
include "colors.inc"
include "texture.inc"

//a light source
light <-10, 10, -10>
```

```
//the ground
//object {
// disc <0,-1,0>,<0,1,0>,0,1000
// texture { checker shiny_red, shiny_blue }
//}

//sphere 1
object {
 sphere <0,0,4>,1
 white_marble
 rotate <0,0,-((frame/total_frames)*(360*6))>
 rotate <0,90+((frame/total_frames)*(360*2)),0>
 translate <-3,0,0>
}

//sphere 2
object {
 sphere <0,0,4>,1
 white_marble
 rotate <0,0,((frame/total_frames)*(360*6))>
 rotate <0,-(frame/total_frames)*(360*2),0>
 translate <3,0,0>
}

//sphere 3
object {
 sphere <0,0,10>,1
 white_marble
 rotate <0,0,((frame/total_frames)*(360*6))>
 rotate <0,-(frame/total_frames)*360,0>
}
```

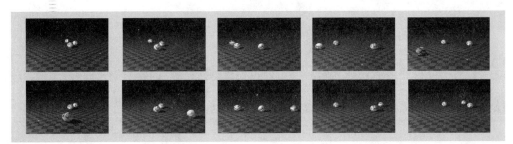

Figure 3-10 The Final Flic

STEP 8: FINAL RENDER

If you're satisfied with the composition of the flic, and you don't need to use your computer for a while, it's time to do a final render. Edit ROLLERS.PI one more time, and change the resolution from "160, 100" to "320, 200." (If you've got a 33-Mhz 80486-based PC or better with Super-VGA, use "640, 480" instead.) Run Polyray one more time, this time in raytrace mode:

```
C:\MOVIES\CHAP3\> polyray rollers.pi -r0 -V1
```

Be warned, this is going to take quite a while; raytracing is much slower than scan-line rendering.

4 ADVANCED TECHNIQUES

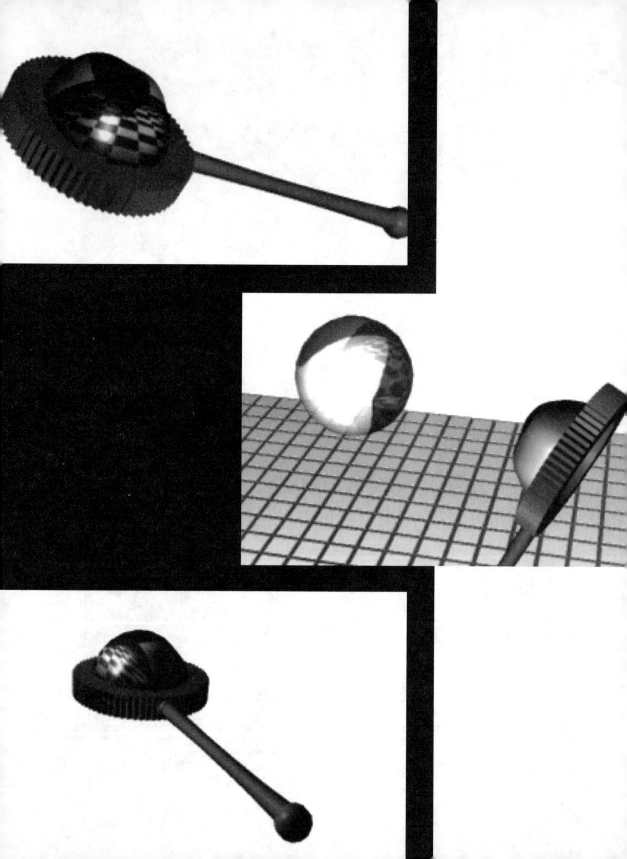

4 ADVANCED TECHNIQUES

Here we focus on ideas and tricks that we breezed past in Chapter 3, *Making a Movie in Eight Steps*. In this chapter, we will explore a number of effects: moving objects, changing the shapes of objects, moving the camera, and changing lighting.

One of the most important tools that we will use is *linear interpolation*. This is a process of changing one value into another following a straight line path. This method is the simplest way to make a change over the course of a series of frames.

For this entire chapter, we will use a standard set of declarations in our data files that help to do the interpolation. These are declarations for starting frame, ending frame, and a calculation of an incremental in-between value. The value of increment will vary from 0 at the first frame to 1 at the end frame. By using this value in our calculations, we will perform linear interpolation. There are often drawbacks to this technique, and many papers have been published describing all of the horrible consequences of doing simple interpolations. However, there are many effects that are quickly and effectively performed with this technique. The format of the declarations will be

```
// Starting and ending frames of the animation
start_frame 0
end_frame 20
// Key times in the animation
define t0 start_frame
define t1 end_frame
// Percent completed between t0 and t1
define increment (frame - t0) / (t1 - t0)
```

The start_frame and end_frame statements are Polyray declarations that define how many frames to render as well as what numbers we want to associate with the start frame and the end frame. Normally, we just use 0 for start_frame and one less than the total number of frames we want as end_frame. The value of the Polyray internal variable frame will take on successive values from start_frame to end_frame as each image in the sequence is rendered. By increasing the value of end_frame, the animation is smoothed out.

In standard terms, we have defined two *keyframes* as t0 and t1. The process of interpolating between keyframes is called *in-betweening* or *tweening*. With these statements (or ones very similar) at the top of a data file, we can then use the value of increment throughout the data file so the tweening will be performed automatically for us. The variables t0 and t1 can be thought of as the start time and end time of the animation. Although we used 0 and 20 in the header above, any two values will do (as long as end_frame is greater than start_frame).

The value increment takes on fractional values between 0 and 1 as each frame is rendered. The nice thing about using this sort of technique is that we can start with a small value of end_frames when first rendering the animation and then use a larger value when we generate the final. That way you can generate a coarse animation with a few frames for testing, then generate a smooth animation with many frames as the final version. The calculations we just did allow Polyray to automatically generate all the correct in-between values.

As a very simple example, Listing 4-1 shows how to make a sphere that varies in size from 1 unit radius to 5 units radius during the course of an animation. Following the header shown above, add the following statements:

LISTING 4-1 BLOATO.PI

```
// Here we define a viewpoint from which we will look at the sphere. This
// declaration puts the camera 10 units behind the origin, and points the
// camera right at the origin (which is where we will put the sphere).
viewpoint {
    from <0, 0, -10>
    at <0, 0, 0>
    up <0, 1, 0>
    resolution 80, 80
    }

// Define a light source - without one everything would be real dark. This
// declaration puts the light above, to the left, and a little behind the
// camera.
light <-10, 10, -15>

// Make a sphere that increases in size.  This declaration creates a sphere
// at the origin (which is <0, 0, 0>) and defines its radius as starting
```

```
// at 1 unit and increasing to 5 units.
object {
    sphere <0, 0, 0>, 1 + increment * 4
    }
```

To render BLOAT0.PI, assemble an animation, and play the animation, following the same steps as previous chapters:

```
C:> polyray bloat0.pi
... frames are rendered ...
C:> dta out*.tga
C:> play anim.fli
```

What you see in this animation looks sort of like a white balloon being inflated. A few frames from the sequence are shown in Figure 4-1. Nothing spectacular, but we have just built an animation that does something very specific between two key points. If you want to make the animation smoother or coarser (add or remove frames), then try changing the value of end_frame to 5 or 50.

MOVING OBJECTS

Suppose you want to move from one place to another over the course of several frames. This section describes several ways to do it, as well as some prepackaged formulas to help you out. In all of the examples, we will start the movement at frame t0, and end the movement at frame t1.

We will explore the following types of movement:

■◀ Along a line

■◀ Around in circles

Figure 4-1 Increasing Radius of a Sphere

◄█ Along a parabola

◄█ Along a spline path

For several of the example animations in this section, we will use an `in-clude` file called STDVIEW.INC shown in Listing 4-2. This file contains some useful declarations: a viewpoint, a light, the background color, a checkered disk that represents the ground, and an object shaped like an arrow.

LISTING 4-2 STDVIEW.INC

```
// Set up the camera
viewpoint {
    from <0,0,-15>
    at <0,0,0>
    up <0,1,0>
    angle 35
    resolution 160, 120
    aspect 4/3
    }

background <0, 0, 0>
light <-10,30, -20>

include "colors.inc"

object {
    disc <0, -5.001, 0>, <0, 1, 0>, 30
    texture { checker matte_white, matte_black }
    }

// Straight arrow of length 3 laying right in the x-axis.  The base of the
// arrow is at the origin, the tip of the arrow is at <3, 0, 0>
define arrow
object {
      object { disc <0, 0, 0>, <-1, 0, 0>, 0.25 }
    + object { cylinder <0, 0, 0>, <2, 0, 0>, 0.25 }
    + object { disc <2, 0, 0>, <1, 0, 0>, 0.25, 0.5 }
    + object { cone <2, 0, 0>, 0.5, <3, 0, 0>, 0 }
    }
```

This file also includes another file, COLORS.INC. This second `include` file defines a number of standard surface colors for objects. The references to `matte_white`, `matte_black`, and `shiny_red` in STDVIEW.INC are all declared in COLORS.INC.

MOVING ALONG A LINE

Suppose you want to move an object from point pos0 to point pos1. A graphical depiction of the movement can be seen in Figure 4-2. At time t0 the object is at position pos0, and at time t1 the object is at position pos1.

The quickest way to move between two points is along a straight line. Calculating each of the points on the line is very easy. Assuming that we have defined pos0 and pos1 as two points:

```
define pos0 <-3, -2, -4>
define pos1 <4, 3, 2>
```

then we can move from pos0 to pos1 using the variable increment from above. The point that we will want to be at for each frame is calculated with the following declaration:

```
define pos (pos0 + increment * (pos1 - pos0))
```

If the object is built at the origin, then the motion from pos0 to pos1 is performed by adding the statement translate pos to the object definition. (Notice that if we use this formula for frame numbers outside the given range, then the object will be located somewhere before pos0 or after pos1 on the line.)

Listing 4-3 shows the file LINE.PI, which demonstrates movement of a sphere along a line.

Figure 4-2 Movement Along a Line

LISTING 4-3 LINE.PI

```
// Move a sphere along a straight line path.

start_frame 0
end_frame 20

// We will use the full 20 frames defined above for the animation
define t0 start_frame
define t1 end_frame

// Figure out how far along we are in the animation
define increment (frame - t0) / (t1 - t0)

include "stdview.inc"

// Define some values for the movement
define pos0 <-3, -2, -4>
define pos1 <4, 3, 2>

// Calculate the current position
define pos pos0 + increment * (pos1 - pos0)

//
// Now move the object
//
object {
   sphere <0, 0.5, 0>, 0.5
   shiny_red
   translate pos
   }
```

For the best effect, assemble this animation using the ping-pong option (/P) in DTA (see Chapter 5, *Movie-Making Tools,* for DTA options). The statements to render the frames and assemble the animation are

```
C:> polyray line.pi
... each frame in the sequence is rendered ...
C:> dta out*.tga /p
```

This will create a flic file called ANIM.FLI. By using the ping-pong option, the ball will appear to bounce back and forth between the two points pos0 and pos1.

MOVING IN CIRCLES

There are several ways we can move in circles. Two basic ways are by translating the object using simple trigonometry, and by rotating the object with the rotate statement. There are times to use each of these, and in this section we will see the differences between the two methods.

The first way uses a little trigonometry to get around. Moving around a circle using the functions `sin` and `cos` is really pretty easy. Suppose you want to move an object in a circular path in the x-y plane, then the statements to do the movement would be

```
define angle radians(increment * 360)
define pos <cos(angle), sin(angle), 0>
```

The resulting movement would follow the path shown in Figure 4-3. In that image, you are looking along the positive *z*-axis, so that only the *x*- and *y*-axes appear in the diagram. The *z*-axis points straight into the page.

The sample file ROTATE1.PI, shown in Listing 4-4, demonstrates movement using the trig functions `sin` and `cos`. In this example, the circle that we move on has a radius of 3. The location on the perimeter of the circle is calculated by using `increment` times the number of degrees in a circle. This tells us how far around we have gone. In order to use the trig functions in Polyray, we have to convert from degrees to radians. Radians are another way of measuring angles. There are just over 6.2 radians in a circle as compared with 360 degrees in a circle. The conversion is performed using the Polyray function `radians`. Once the angle is known, we generate the final location by using `sin` and `cos` functions.

Figure 4-3 Positive Rotation Using Sin/Cos

LISTING 4-4 ROTATE1.PI

```
// Start with definitions of frame counts, increment, viewpoint and light
start_frame 0
end_frame 19
define t0 start_frame
define t1 end_frame+1
define increment (frame - t0) / (t1 - t0)
// Include a predefined viewpoint, light source, etc.
include "stdview.inc"

// Here we define the radius of the circle, followed by the
// position on the circle.
define radius 3
define ang radians(increment * 360)
define pos radius * <cos(ang), 0, sin(ang)>

// We now take an arrow that is defined in stdview.inc and translate
// it into the position we just calculated.
arrow {
    shiny_red
    translate pos
    }
```

A corresponding sample file that uses `rotate` to move a sphere in a circle is found in ROTATE2.PI, shown in Listing 4-5. The only differences between the two files are the last few lines of the file. In this example, we first move the arrow out to the circle's perimeter with the statement `translate <2, 0, 0>`, then we rotate the arrow around the y-axis with the statement `rotate <0, ang, 0>`.

LISTING 4-5 ROTATE2.PI

```
// Start with definitions of frame counts, increment, viewpoint and light
start_frame 0
end_frame 19
define t0 start_frame
define t1 end_frame+1
define increment (frame - t0) / (t1 - t0)
// Include a predefined viewpoint, light source, etc.
include "stdview.inc"

// Calculate the rotation angle
define ang increment * 360

// We now take an arrow that is defined in stdview.inc and rotate
// it into position
arrow {
```

```
shiny_red
translate <2, 0, 0>
rotate <0, pos, 0>
translate <0, 0, 5>
}
```

Using the `rotate` statement can be somewhat subtle. The rotation in Polyray is left-handed. To visualize how the rotation works: point along the axis of rotation with the thumb of your left hand so your fingers curl in the positive direction of rotation. A sample image depicting the positive directions of rotation about the three axes is shown in Figure 4-4. In that image, the *x*-axis points to the right, the *y*-axis points up, and the *z*-axis points away (into the page). That image is part of an animation that rotates the circular arrows in their positive directions of motion. The data file for that animation is ROTATE3.PI.

There are a couple of things you need to remember when setting up movement in a circle. The functions `sin` and `cos` need to have their angles in radians. The `rotate` statement needs to have its angles in degrees. If you inadvertently use an angle in degrees in either `sin` or `cos`, you will move through angles much larger than you really wanted.

Figure 4-4 Positive Directions of Rotation

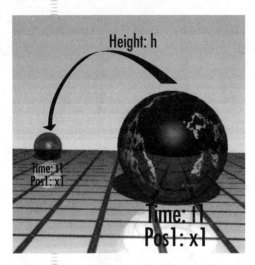

Figure 4-5 Movement Along a Parabola

MOVING ON A PARABOLA

One sort of path that is useful when trying to simulate the way things bounce is a parabola. Bouncing balls naturally follow this sort of curve, due to the influence of gravity. A diagram of a parabolic path can be seen in Figure 4-5.

As before, we will move an object along a path from pos0 to pos1. In order to simplify things, we will stick to two dimensions for awhile. Points pos0 and pos1 will both lie on the *x*-axis, with pos0 at position x0 and pos1 at position x1. The motion of the parabola will go up and down along the *y*-axis. We won't move in the *z*-axis at all. The variable height will be used for the height of the top of the parabola. Given these variables, we can easily figure out the motion.

To demonstrate how the movement can be calculated, the following data file moves a sphere along a parabola. The file is included as parab.pi, and shown in Listing 4-6.

LISTING 4-6 PARAB.PI

```
// Move a sphere along a parabola

start_frame 0
end_frame 20
```

```
// We will use the full 20 frames defined above for the animation
//
define t0 start_frame
define t1 end_frame
//
// Figure out how far along we are in the animation
//
define increment (frame - t0) / (t1 - t0)

include "stdview.inc"

// Define some values for the movement
define x0 -3
define x1 3
define height 8

// Now do the calculation
define x_pos x0 + increment * (x1 - x0)
define y_pos 4 * height * (x_pos - x0) * (x1 - x_pos) / (x1 - x0)^2

// Now move the object
object {
    sphere <0, -4.5, 0>, 0.5 // Sphere is placed on the ground plane
    shiny_red
    translate <x_pos, y_pos, 5>
    }
```

This animation should be assembled using the ping-pong option in DTA so the ball will bounce back and forth.

MOVING ALONG A SPLINE PATH

As previously mentioned, linear interpolation between values doesn't always give the best-looking results. One way to address this is to use *splines*. The formulas for the splines we use are a little more complex than the lines and circles we just used.

In this example, we will be moving between the same points that we did in the straight line example. The difference is that in this case we will also define how fast the object is moving at each of these points, as well as the direction of the movement. There is a very simple way to model this sort of movement, and it uses a spline to connect the points.

There are many types of spline curves, the one we will demonstrate in this section is called a *cubic spline*. In order to make a path for the object to follow, you need to know four pieces of information:

- ▶ Starting location of the object
- ▶ Starting velocity of the object
- ▶ Ending location of the object
- ▶ Ending velocity of the object

A diagram of a spline curve and its associated information is shown in Figure 4-6.

Velocity here needs to be more than just how fast the object is moving—we also need to know in which direction the movement will be occurring.

Here are the calculations needed to create the spline. Note that the definitions of u, a0, ..., a3 are independent of any particular object's movement. They only depend on the value of increment. If you want to have a number of objects following spline paths during the same set of frames, you only need to define these values once. For those interested in the math behind these equations, refer to Rogers and Adams' *Mathematical Elements for Computer Graphics*. For our purposes, it is sufficient to know that if increment varies between 0 and 1 over a set of frames, then the value of pos will smoothly move between pos0 and pos1 over the same set of frames.

```
define u  increment
define u2 (u * u)
define u3 (u2 * u)
define a0 (2 * u3 - 3 * u2 + 1)
define a1 (-2 * u3 + 3 * u2)
define a2 (u3 - 2 * u2 + u)
define a3 (u3 - u2)
```

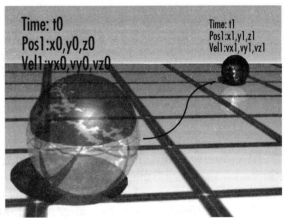

Time: t0
Pos1:x0,y0,z0
Vel1:vx0,vy0,vz0

Time: t1
Pos1:x1,y1,z1
Vel1:vx1,vy1,vz1

Figure 4-6 Movement Along a Spline Curve

The actual position of the object during the animation is now calculated by using the values of a0, ..., a3:

```
define pos (a0 * pos0 + a1 * pos1 + a2 * vel0 + a3 * vel1)
```

Listing 4-7 (SPLINE1.PI) demonstrates movement of a sphere along a spline curve. This file has the same sort of header information we have been using all along in this chapter, including the definition of the length of the animation, the definition of the key times t0 and t1 in the animation, and inclusion of STDVIEW.INC.

LISTING 4-7 SPLINE1.PI

```
// Move a sphere along a spline path.
start_frame 0
end_frame 40

// We will use the full 40 frames defined above for the animation
define t0 start_frame
define t1 end_frame

// Figure how far along we are in the animation
define increment (frame - t0) / (t1 - t0)

// Get the standard view setup
include "stdview.inc"

// Define some values for the movement
define pos0 <-3, -2, -4>
define vel0 <20, 0, -3>
define pos1 <4, 3, 2>
define vel1 <0, 30, 20>

// Calculate the various coefficients of the spline path
define u   increment
define u2 (u * u)
define u3 (u2 * u)
define a0 (2 * u3 - 3 * u2 + 1)
define a1 (-2 * u3 + 3 * u2)
define a2 (u3 - 2 * u2 + u)
define a3 (u3 - u2)

// Finally the position is calculated from the coefficients:
define pos (a0 * pos0 + a1 * pos1 + a2 * vel0 + a3 * vel1)

// Now create the sphere and move it into position
object {
```

```
sphere <0, 0.5, 0>, 0.5
shiny_red
translate pos
}
```

Following the boilerplate header, we have the definitions of the start and end positions of the sphere together with the starting and ending velocities. Notice that the *x* component of `vel0` is very large compared to the *y* and *z* values. This results in the motion of the sphere at the beginning of the spline (which is at the beginning of the animation) to be from left to right. The high values of the *y* and *z* components in `vel1` cause the motion of the sphere at the end of the spline to be upwards and away from the viewpoint.

ORIENTATION ON A SPLINE PATH

Next we tackle a slightly more difficult problem. Suppose we want to turn an object as we move it along a spline path. How do we get the object into the proper orientation?

There are two approaches to doing this. The first is to design the object in a particular orientation, rotate it into the correct orientation, and then translate it to the final position. The other approach is to define the object along the desired orientation. For the latter approach, we will redefine the arrow in STDVIEW.INC along the direction of travel.

Determining the direction of the velocity is pretty simple if we use the values calculated above for the spline path. The values of `a0` and `a1` are what determine how far along the spline we happen to be. By using these values to determine the intermediate velocity, we can figure out the direction of motion. The following excerpts from SPLINE2.PI (Listing 4-8) and SPLINE3.PI (Listing 4-9) show how to calculate the information needed to incorporate orientation into movement along a spline path.

```
define increment_vel (a0 * vel0 + a1 * vel1)
define norm_vel increment_vel / fabs(increment_vel)
```

The vector `norm_vel` has a length of 1 and points in the direction of the velocity along the spline curve. We now use this direction to get the arrow into the proper orientation. For the first approach, which is orienting the object and then translating the object into position, the definition would be

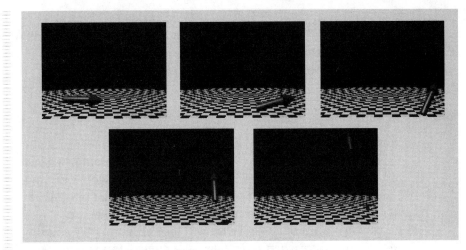

Figure 4-7 Spline Path Example

LISTING 4-8 SPLINE2.PI

```
define half_angle (norm_vel + <1, 0, 0>) / 2
//
// Make an arrow in the appropriate direction
//
arrow {
    rotate half_angle, 180
    shiny_red
    translate pos
    }
```

For the second approach, in which we actually build the arrow along the final direction, the definition of the object would be

LISTING 4-9 SPLINE3.PI

```
//
// Make an arrow in the appropriate direction
//
object {
      object { disc <0, 0, 0>, -norm_vel, 0.25 }
    + object { cylinder <0, 0, 0>, 2*norm_vel, 0.25 }
    + object { disc 2*norm_vel, norm_vel, 0.25, 0.5 }
    + object { cone 2*norm_vel, 0.5, 3*norm_vel, 0 }
    shiny_red
    translate pos
    }
```

Both SPLINE2.PI and SPLINE3.PI result in identical animations. A sequence of frames showing an arrow following a spline curve are shown in Figure 4-7. Note how the arrow changes its direction as it travels.

TEXTURE TRICKS

Texturing is a way of simulating intricate surface detail and coloration. *Solid texturing* refers to the use of three-dimensional functions to build textures. This section presents a few ways of doing tricks with texturing. We don't have the space to go into a lot of detail, so for further information see Chapter 5, *Movie-Making Tools,* and the Polyray documents.

The first form of a texture we will look at is a marble coloring. Marble is formed in nature when several layers of mineral form on top of each other. If the layers are somewhat liquid, they can swirl into each other. The sample file TURB1.PI shows a sphere with a marble texture. At the beginning of the animation, the marble has very straight even layers. As the animation progresses, the marble layers start to mix more and more.

The colors of the marble will be white and black. To define how the colors change through the layers of the texture, we use a color map. The Polyray function that builds these maps is called, logically enough, `color_map`. This

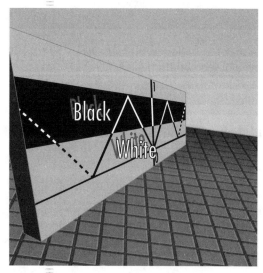

Figure 4-8 Sawtooth Function

Figure 4-9 Sawtooth with Noise Added

function is a way of specifying a color based on a texturing function.

Because we want to repeat the layers one after another, we need to be able to fold positions on the *x*-axis so that any position will result in a lookup value that is within the bounds of the color map. To do this, we use the function `sawtooth`. The sawtooth function looks like a set of triangles one after another. The diagram in Figure 4-8 shows its shape and how we will associate its values with colors. By plugging the *x* value of an object into the function, we get a number from 0 to 1 back out.

If we just used the sawtooth function and the color map alone, we would get very even layers of coloring. However, if you look at natural marble, the layers tend to swirl around. To simulate this swirling, we add a little randomness. The randomness is provided by the function `noise`. Adding noise to the sawtooth function results in a new function that appears something like the one in Figure 4-9. This process is often referred to as *turbulence*.

The amount of the extra wiggling added to the original sawtooth is what determines the amount of swirl in the layers of marble. TURB1.PI, shown in Listing 4-10, starts with no noise and progressively adds more and more. When the animation is played you see the layers start to fold and bend.

The important items to look at in the data file below are the definition of the color map, the definition of the marble function, and how these are put together in the marble texture. For more details on how the `special surface` declaration works, see Chapter 5, *Movie-Making Tools*.

LISTING 4-10 TURB1.PI

```
// Animated texture:  more and more turbulence in the veins of a white
// marble sphere
start_frame 0
end_frame 20
define t0 0
define t1 end_frame

// Figure out how far along we are in the animation
define increment (frame - t0) / (t1 - t0)

// Set up the camera
viewpoint {
   from <0, 0, -8>
   at <0,0,0>
   up <0,1,0>
   angle 45
   resolution 80, 80
   }


background midnightblue
light 0.7*white, <-10, 3, -20>
light 0.7*white, < 10, 3, -20>

// The layers of marble are stacked along the x-axis and wiggled by
// the noise function
define marble_fn sawtooth(P[0] + 3*increment*noise(P, 2))

// Define the colors of the layers in the marble
define white_marble_map
   color_map([0.0, 0.8, white, <0.6,0.6,0.6>]
             [0.8, 1.0, <0.6, 0.6, 0.6>, <0.1, 0.1, 0.1>])

// Put together the marble texture from the color map and the
// marble function
define white_marble1
texture {
   special surface {
      color white_marble_map[marble_fn]
      ambient 0.2
      diffuse 0.7
      specular white, 0.5
      microfacet Phong 10
      }
   }

// Make the marble sphere
object { sphere <0, 0, 0>, 2 white_marble }
```

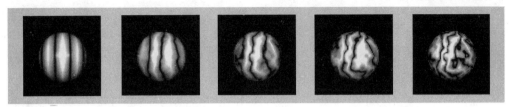

Figure 4-10 Animating Turbulence

Several frames from this animation are shown in Figure 4-10. The starting frame has very even layers of black and white. By the end of the sequence, the bands have been greatly twisted about.

Our next example demonstrates a sort of dissolve effect. By modifying the transparency of an object, we can make parts of its surface disappear. This time the function we use divides the object into layers in both the *x* and *y* directions. The result is a sort of wireframe appearance.

The key to how this works is the definition of `wire_exper`. This function tests the distance of each point on the surface of the sphere to see how close it is to evenly spaced values along the *x*- and *y*-axes. If the distance is less than `density`, then the point is visible. If the distance is more than `density`, then the point is transparent. The value of `freq` is what determines how closely spaced the wires will be.

The declaration of `wire_red` uses `wire_exper` in several places. It is used to define the color of the surface, resulting in red where `wire_exper` determines that it should be visible. The texture will be completely transparent everywhere else. See Listing 4-11 for a sample file.

LISTING 4-11 WIRE.PI

```
// A wireframe dissolve effect

start_frame 0
end_frame 60

define t0 0
define t1 end_frame
define increment (frame - t0) / (t1 - t0)

// Set up the camera
viewpoint {
    from <0,5,-7>
    at <0,0,0>
    up <0,1,0>
    angle 45
```

continued on next page

continued from previous page

```
    resolution 80, 80
    }

background <0, 0, 0>
light <-10, 20, -20>

include "colors.inc"

define density increment
define freq 3

// wire_exper returns 1 if we are on the visible part of the surface,
// and returns 0 if we are on the see-through part of the surface.
define wire_exper (|fmod(freq * P[0], 1)| < density ? 1
                    : (|fmod(freq * P[1], 1)| < density ? 1 : 0))

// Build the texture from the function wire_exper
define wire_red
texture {
    special surface {
        color wire_exper * red
        ambient 0.1
        diffuse 0.4
        specular wire_exper * white, 0.5
        microfacet Reitz 10
        transmission white, 1 - wire_exper, 1.0
        }
    }

// Attach the texture to a sphere
object { sphere <0, 0, 0>, 2 wire_red }
```

A few frames from this animation can be seen in Figure 4-11. At one extreme the sphere is totally invisible, at the other the sphere is totally solid. The wireframe nature of the dissolve can be seen in the intermediate frames.

The last example of texture animation combines the ideas of the two previous examples. We will use a color map and turbulence to simulate a flame.

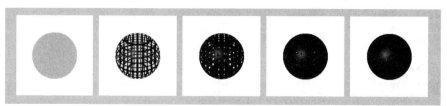

Figure 4-11 Wireframe Dissolve

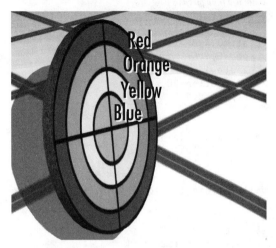

Figure 4-12 Arrangement of Flame Colors

In addition, we will use transparency to modify the edges of the flame so we can see through the edges.

The color map for the flame uses several colors that are observed inside a flame: blue at the hot part in the middle, followed by yellow, then orange, then red at the edges. The function we use to determine the colors is shaped like an ellipse, where the distance from the center of the ellipse is used to look up values from the color map. The structure of the ellipse and its associated colors is diagramed in Figure 4-12.

To give the flame a flickering appearance, we will add some turbulence to the ellipse. The turbulence will change the edges of the ellipse in a manner similar to the way the sawtooth function was modified above. The definition of flame_fn simply adds together the definition of distance from the center of an ellipse with the noise function. Notice that within the noise function we add an offset to the position variable P. This is what causes the shape of the flame to change just a little bit from frame to frame. FLAME.PI, shown in Listing 4-12, takes a bit longer than other samples to compile.

LISTING 4-12 FLAME.PI

```
// Flickering flame animation
start_frame 0
end_frame 300
```

continued on next page

continued from previous page

```
viewpoint {
   from <0,3,-14>
   at <0,4,0>
   up <0,1,0>
   angle 45
   resolution 80, 160
   aspect 0.5
   }


background midnight_blue
light < 5, 10, -20>
include "colors.inc"

define flame_fn (sqrt(1.5 * x^2 + y^2) +
                     2 * noise(P + <0, -frame/3, frame/6>, 1))
define flame_tex
texture {
   special surface {
      ambient 1
      diffuse 0
      specular 0
      transmission (flame_fn < 5 ? black
                    : (flame_fn > 8 ? white
                         : white * (flame_fn - 5) / 3)), 1, 1
      color color_map([-50, 1, blue, blue]
                   [1, 2, blue, yellow]
                   [2, 3, yellow, yellow]
                   [3, 4, yellow, orange]
                   [4, 5, orange, red]
                   [5, 8, red, black]
                   [8, 20, black, black], blue)[flame_fn]
      }
   }

object {
   sphere <0, 4.5, 0>, 5
   scale <2/5, 1, 1/100>
   flame_tex { translate <0, 0.5, 0> }
   }
```

Figure 4-13 shows a sequence of frames from the animation. Each frame changes just slightly from the last. The features within the flame move as the animation progresses.

Using texturing for surface detail and animating the textures is a very compact way to get effects. Indeed, some effects would be extremely difficult to generate if a model needed to be built. The previous flame example is one case in point. To model the shapes that a flame takes on as it flickers would be very difficult. To simulate the coloring of a flickering flame is much easier.

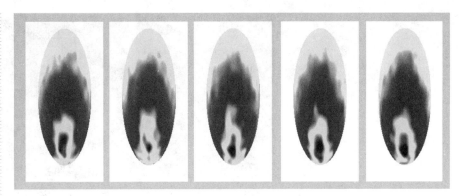

Figure 4-13 Animated Flame Texture

COMPLEX PATHS

During the course of an animation, you may want to have an object follow a sequence of paths, rather than just a single one. The next couple of sections describe how an animation can be built up from a set of keyframe data, and how you can perform separate interpolations between each set of keys. Two typical examples are given, a set of straight line paths and a sequence of spline paths.

MULTIPLE STRAIGHT LINE PATHS

The easiest sequence to follow is a set of straight lines. By defining a set of keyframes, we can split movement across the individual lines by interpolating between the start and end points of each segment. The key here is to make sure you allocate enough frames to each segment so that the motion between two points doesn't happen at a different speed than between two other points.

Figure 4-14 shows how we can split a set of moves into keyframes. In this example, there are keyframes at each of four times: t0, t1, t2, and t3.

Once you have assigned times to each of the points you want to pass through, the next step is to decide how you are going to move between each point. Listing 4-13 (LINES.PI) will move an object from the start to the end with a specific number of frames for each move.

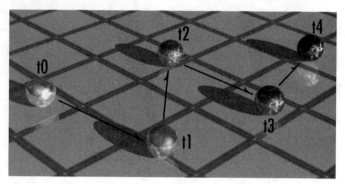

Figure 4-14 Following a Series of Line Segments

LISTING 4-13 LINES.PI

```
// Move a sphere along a series of line segments

// First we define the key locations that we will move through
define key_pos [<-3, -2, -4>, <4, -2, -4>, <-1, 2, 0>,
                <2, -1, -1>, <4, 3, 2>]

// Next define how long it takes to move from one point to another
define moves_per_frame [7, 6, 5, 8]

// Define the starting and ending frames of each segment, based on the
// number of frames it takes to execute each segment
define start_times [0, moves_per_frame[0],
                    moves_per_frame[0] + moves_per_frame[1],
                    moves_per_frame[0] + moves_per_frame[1] +
                    moves_per_frame[2]]
define end_times [start_times[1], start_times[2], start_times[3],
                  start_times[3] + moves_per_frame[3]]

// Now define the length of the entire animation as the frame number of
// the last move
start_frame 0
end_frame end_times[3]
total_frames end_frame

if (frame < end_times[0])
   define segment 0
```

```
else if (frame < end_times[1])
   define segment 1
else if (frame < end_times[2])
   define segment 2
else
   define segment 3

define t0 start_times[segment]
define t1 end_times[segment]

// Figure out how far along we are in the animation
define increment (frame - t0) / (t1 - t0)

include "stdview.inc"

// Calculate the position of the sphere
define pos key_pos[segment] +
         increment * (key_pos[segment+1] - key_pos[segment])

// Now move the object
object {
   sphere <0, 0.5, 0>, 0.5
   shiny_red
   translate pos
   }
```

After that set of declarations, the position "pos" is where the object will be placed. Shown below is a sphere that is being moved along the sequence of line segments. The sphere is shown at each of the keyframe locations. The key points in the animation file can be seen in Figure 4-15.

Figure 4-15 Sphere Moving Along a Series of Line Segments

MULTIPLE SPLINE PATHS

For the ultimate in smooth movement across a series of keyframes, a set of connected spline paths can be used. It's a bit tougher to build the connecting information, but the result can be a very nice movement.

The essential process is the same as connecting line segments. We need to identify key locations, and in order to make the splines work right, we also need to define a set of key velocities. Figure 4-16 shows how we can make a figure-eight out of a set of four spline curves.

This is as far as we will take splines here. For a slightly more complex example, see Chapter 6, *The Movie Pages,* for an example of an object flying a figure-eight by using splines.

WEIRD MATH

Mathematics is a rich source of formulas that we can animate in one way or another. All the functions that get piled onto us during Trigonometry classes are likely candidates for making an animation. The sample here is called a sombrero surface, due to the resemblance to a Mexican hat. It also resembles, in some ways, the surface of water after a drop hits it.

We will vary the phase of the function of this surface. Because the base wavy part of the surface is based on the cosine function, all we need to do is make the angle vary from 0 to 360 degrees in order to create a nice looping animation.

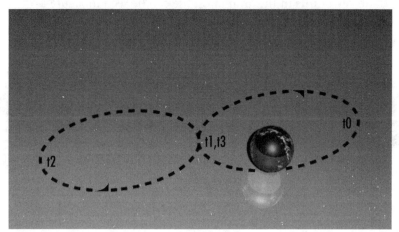

Figure 4-16 Following a Figure-Eight Course as a Series of Four Splines

The formula for the function is

```
c * cos(-phase + two_pi * a * sqrt(x^2 + z^2)) * exp(-b * sqrt(x^2 + z^2))
```

By choosing values for a, b, and c, and varying the value of **phase**, we will have our moving surface. The object in Polyray that we use to generate the surface is called a *height field*. This object is represented by a grid of triangles, with the corners of the triangles corresponding to elevation. Height fields are used for fractal mountains, the surface of water, and (as we are doing here) to represent math functions.

The sample file SOMBRERO.PI is shown in Listing 4-14. This animation uses the function described above as the argument to a Polyray height field. Polyray internally builds a model of the function. We modify the phase value, causing the bumps on the surface to appear to move.

LISTING 4-14 SOMBRERO.PI

```
// Animation of a sombrero surface
start_frame 0
end_frame 19

// Set up the camera
viewpoint {
    from <0, 5, -8>
    at <0, 0, 0>
    up <0,1,0>
    angle 40
    resolution 80, 80
    }

// Get various surface finishes
include "colors.inc"

// Set up background color & lights
background midnightblue
light <10,10,-10>

// Define the start and end points of the animation
define t0 start_frame
define t1 end_frame+1

// Figure out how far along we are in the animation
define increment (frame - t0) / (t1 - t0)

// Animate the surface by changing the phase of the function
define ang radians(increment * 360)
```

continued on next page

continued from previous page

```
// Define constants for the sombrero function
define a_const 1.0
define b_const 1.0
define c_const 3.0
define two_pi_a 2.0 * 3.14159265358 * a_const

define shiny_white
texture {
    surface {
        ambient white, 0.2
        diffuse white, 0.6
        specular white, 0.3
        microfacet Reitz 10
        }
    }

// Define a diminishing cosine surface (sombrero)
object {
    height_fn 80, 80, -4, 4, -4, 4,
        c_const * cos(-ang + two_pi_a * sqrt(x^2 + z^2)) *
                        exp(-b_const * sqrt(x^2 + z^2))
    shiny_white
    }
```

Figure 4-17 shows a set of frames from the animated sombrero surface.

3-D MORPHS

One of the hot trends in TV commercials today is "morphing." Video games that turn into CDs, heads that become cubical, dancing teakettles.... Some of these effects are strictly 2-D—the artists perform transformations on images. Others involve modeling 3-D objects that change shape. This section deals with one of the simpler forms of morphing 3-D objects.

Figure 4-17 Animated Sombrero Surface

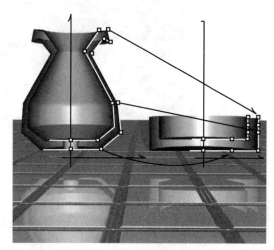

Figure 4-18 Cross Section Design
of Lathe Surfaces

Certain types of shape transformations are easy to do in Polyray. Polyray supports a *lathe* object, in which it revolves a polygon about an axis. This sort of object is also referred to as a *surface of revolution*. Examples of objects that have this property are wineglasses and vases. In Polyray this type of object is specified by a set of control points that trace out its cross section.

If you have two surfaces of revolution, it is reasonably easy to change one into the other. To do this, we interpolate between the control points of the first surface and the control points of the second surface. The next example shows how to change smoothly from a vase into a tumbler.

The first step is to design the cross section of the two shapes you are going to move between. To make things easy, you should use exactly the same number of control points in the first surface as in the second.

The figure below shows the arrangement of the control points of two lathe surfaces. Although the border is made up of straight lines in the design, Polyray will be able to round off the corners, giving a smooth shape. During the course of the animation, each control point in the first surface will be moved toward a corresponding control point in the second surface. In Figure 4-18, the association of a couple of the control points is shown. The corresponding surfaces that the diagrams build are shown in Figure 4-19.

Figure 4-19 Rendered Images of Lathe Surfaces

First, we must assign coordinates to each of the control points. The easiest way to do this is to do your design on graph paper, then simply count along the axes on the graph paper to figure out what numbers you need. The 12 coordinates for the vase and the tumbler are defined in the data file as `vase_points` and `mug_points`.

Once we have the starting and ending shapes defined, we need to tell Polyray how to make the shapes that come in between. This is done by defining a lathe shape using coordinates that are interpolated from the start to the end. We use `increment` to linearly interpolate between each pair of coordinates. The object definition contains 12 equations that perform the interpolation for each individual point in the definitions of the vase and the mug, as seen in Listing 4-15.

LISTING 4-15 MORPH1.PI

```
// Transformation from a vase to a mug
start_frame 0
end_frame 20

// Set up the camera
viewpoint {
   from <0,5,-15>
   at <0,0,0>
   up <0,1,0>
   angle 35
   resolution 160, 120
   aspect 4/3
   }

background <0, 0, 0>
light <-10,30, -20>

include "colors.inc"
```

```
define t0 0
define t1 end_frame
define increment (frame - t0) / (t1 - t0)

// Define the outline of the starting and ending shapes
define vase_points [<0, 0>, <2, 0>, <3, 1>, <3, 2>, <1, 7>, <2.5, 8>,
                    <2, 8>, <0.5, 7>, <2.5, 2>, <2.5, 1>, <2, 0.5>, <0, 0.5>]
define mug_points [<0, 0>, <2, 0>, <2, 1>, <2, 2>, <2, 3>, <2, 4>,
                   <1.5, 4>, <1.5, 3>, <1.5, 2>, <1.5, 1>, <1.5, 0.5>, <0, 0.5>]

// Make a lathe surface that morphs between a vase and a tumbler
object {
    lathe 2, <0, 1, 0>, 12,
        vase_points[0] + increment * (mug_points[0] - vase_points[0]),
        vase_points[1] + increment * (mug_points[1] - vase_points[1]),
        vase_points[2] + increment * (mug_points[2] - vase_points[2]),
        vase_points[3] + increment * (mug_points[3] - vase_points[3]),
        vase_points[4] + increment * (mug_points[4] - vase_points[4]),
        vase_points[5] + increment * (mug_points[5] - vase_points[5]),
        vase_points[6] + increment * (mug_points[6] - vase_points[6]),
        vase_points[7] + increment * (mug_points[7] - vase_points[7]),
        vase_points[8] + increment * (mug_points[8] - vase_points[8]),
        vase_points[9] + increment * (mug_points[9] - vase_points[9]),
        vase_points[10] + increment * (mug_points[10] - vase_points[10]),
        vase_points[11] + increment * (mug_points[11] - vase_points[11])
    translate <0, -5, 5>
    u_steps 16
    }

// Ground floor
object {
    disc <0, -5.001, 0>, <0, 1, 0>, 30
    texture { checker matte_white, matte_black scale <2, 2, 2> }
    }
```

The resulting set of shapes can be seen in the sequence that is shown in Figure 4-20. Even though we used the simplest possible means of transforming the control points of the lathe, we still get a very smooth transforma-

Figure 4-20 Transformation from a Vase into a Tumbler

tion from one shape to another. The next step is, of course, creating morphs like those in *Terminator 2*....

LIGHTING, OPTICAL EFFECTS

Up to now, we have concentrated on the process of animating objects. There is quite a bit more that can be animated. For example, you may want to move the eyepoint, change the field of view, or perhaps animate the lighting in the scene. We will explore a couple of these processes.

ANIMATING THE VIEWPOINT

If you've ever played with a movie camera or a video camera, one of the first things you started playing with was the zoom button. Well, Polyray doesn't exactly have a pushbutton to do zooms, but it does support a field of view, referred to in the viewpoint declaration as `angle`. By making the field of view smaller, we do a zoom into a scene; by making the field of view larger, we zoom out.

As a little example, suppose we arrange a few spheres on the ground, as we want to zoom into one (hard to say why, maybe it has a nice color). Then by setting the `at` part of the viewpoint and the `angle` part of the viewpoint, we can get the desired effect. During the animation, we are going to go from a field of view of 60 degrees (fairly wide) to a field of view of 4 degrees (pretty tight). The sample code EYE1.PI is shown in Listing 4-16.

LISTING 4-16 EYE1.PI

```
// Short animation of changing field of view
start_frame 0
end_frame 30

// We will use the full 30 frames defined above for the animation
define t0 start_frame
define t1 end_frame

// Figure out how far along we are in the animation
define increment (frame - t0) / (t1 - t0)

// Define the starting and ending field of view
define start_fov 60
define end_fov 4
```

```
// Make the size of the field of view dependent on where we are in
// the animation
define fov start_fov + increment * (end_fov - start_fov)

// Set up the camera
viewpoint {
    from <4,5,-15>
    at <0,1,0>
    up <0,1,0>
    angle fov
    resolution 160, 120
    aspect 4/3
    }

background <0, 0, 0>
light 0.8*white, <-10, 30, -20>
light 0.8*white, < 10, 30, -20>

include "colors.inc"

// Put some objects into the scene

object { sphere <0, 2, 0>, 2 mirror }

define little_ball object { sphere <0, 1, 0>, 1 }

little_ball { shiny_green    translate <-3.0, 0,-3.0> }
little_ball { shiny_cyan     translate <-3.0, 0, 0.0> }
little_ball { shiny_yellow   translate <-3.0, 0, 3.0> }
little_ball { shiny_magenta  translate < 0.0, 0,-3.0> }
little_ball { shiny_blue     translate < 0.0, 0, 3.0> }
little_ball { shiny_coral    translate < 3.0, 0,-3.0> }
little_ball { shiny_red      translate < 3.0, 0, 0.0> }
little_ball { shiny_orange   translate < 3.0, 0, 3.0> }

// Ground plane
object {
    polygon 4, <-10, 0,-10>, <-10, 0, 10>, < 10, 0, 10>, < 10, 0,-10>
    texture { checker matte_white, matte_black }
    }
```

Following the definition of the viewpoint, we define a few simple objects: a checkerboard, a mirrored sphere at the center, and some colored spheres around the mirrored sphere.

The end result of our zoom can be seen in Figure 4-21. The first frame shows all but a couple of corners of the checkerboard. After we zoom in all

Figure 4-21 Zooming into a Scene

the way, only part of one of the colored spheres is visible, and the rest of the frame is filled with the reflection from the mirrored sphere at the center.

A more general change to the viewpoint is to actually change the location and direction of the camera's view—creating a fly-through of a scene. It can be a little difficult to control the movement and orientation of the camera. But for a real 3-D action sequence, camera movements give an effect that can't be beaten. For example, we will make a forest of arrows pointing up and will move the camera on a straight path between arrows.

In order to keep the size of the animation under control, we will make sure it loops after a very short period of time. Because the arrows will be arranged in an even grid and the ground is a regular checker pattern, we only need to generate enough frames to move forward two checkers. After that point, the scene essentially repeats.

For a more advanced animation, you would have to fit the end of one camera movement to the start of another. This would involve developing spline paths for the camera to follow, and would require very careful attention to speed of movement and orientation of the camera as you pass from one keyframe to another.

Moving the camera in this example involves defining the starting and ending location EYE2.PI of the viewpoint, as well as the direction we are looking. The sample file is shown in Listing 4-17.

LISTING 4-17 EYE2.PI

```
// Short animation of changing field of view
start_frame 0
end_frame 30

// Because the last frame "loops" back to the start, we don't use the
// last frame.
define t0 start_frame
define t1 end_frame-1

// Figure out how far along we are in the animation
define increment (frame - t0) / (t1 - t0)
```

```
define start_eye_location <0, 0.5, 0>
define end_eye_location <0, 0.5, 10>
define eye_location
   start_eye_location + increment * (end_eye_location - start_eye_location)

// Set up the camera
viewpoint {
   from eye_location
   at eye_location + <0, 0, 1>
   up <0,1,0>
   angle 45
   resolution 160, 120
   aspect 4/3
   }

background <0, 0, 0>

// Put the lights way out so that the shading won't change too much
// between the first frame and the last.
light 0.8*white, <-100, 300, -200>
light 0.8*white, < 100, 300, -200>

include "colors.inc"

// Ground plane
object {
   disc <0, 0, 0>, <0, 1, 0>, 500
   texture { checker matte_white, matte_black scale <5, 5, 5> }
   }

// Forest of arrows standing upright
define arrow_y
object {
     object { disc <0, 0, 0>, <-1, 0, 0>, 0.25 }
   + object { cylinder <0, 0, 0>, <2, 0, 0>, 0.25 }
   + object { disc <2, 0, 0>, <1, 0, 0>, 0.25, 0.5 }
   + object { cone <2, 0, 0>, 0.5, <3, 0, 0>, 0 }
   rotate <0, 0, 90>
   shiny_red
   }

define arrow_grid
   object {
      gridded "allblk.tga",
      arrow_y { scale <1/3,1/3,1/3> translate <0.5, 0, 0.5> }
      }
arrow_grid { translate <-32, 0, 0> }
arrow_grid
arrow_grid { translate <-32, 0, 32> }
arrow_grid { translate <  0, 0, 32> }
```

Figure 4-22 Flying Through a Scene

The only tricky thing in this file is the use of a gridded object declaration. This declaration is used by Polyray to perform automatic placement of objects using an image file as the guide. We use it here to create a regular grid of arrows without having to explicitly declare each individual arrow. Further details of this object type are in Chapter 5, *Movie-Making Tools,* and the Polyray documents. Figure 4-22 shows a set of frames from the animation.

ANIMATING LIGHTS

After playing with object placement and shape changes, swirling textures, and zooming and weaving through your scenes, you still need to animate the lighting of the scene. There are a number of properties that can be animated, including color, location, and where the light shines. To demonstrate the sorts of effects that can be acheived with lighting, we will shine three spotlights at separate locations on a wall, then move the direction of the lights until all three lights point at the same location on the floor.

Listing 4-18 shows SPOT1.PI. In this animation, the important declarations are of `spot0_pos`, `spot1_pos`, and `spot2_pos`. These three values are the only things that change. They define the place where the spotlight is pointing.

LISTING 4-18 SPOT.PI

```
// Animation of three spotlights changing the area they illuminate

// Set up the camera
viewpoint {
    from <0,5,-15>
    at <0,2,0>
    up <0,1,0>
    angle 35
    resolution 160, 120
    aspect 4/3
    }

background <0, 0, 0>
light 0.3*white, <-10,30, -20>

include "colors.inc"

start_frame 0
end_frame 20

// We will use the full 20 frames defined above for the animation
define t0 start_frame
define t1 end_frame

// Figure out how far along we are in the animation
define increment (frame - t0) / (t1 - t0)

// Define some values for the movement
define pos0 [<-7, 5, 10>, < 0, 5, 10>, < 7, 5, 10>]
define pos1 [<-1, 0, 0>, < 0, 0, 0>, < 1, 0, 0>]

// We calculate the point_at part of each spotlight with the next three
// statements.  Each one extracts a start and end point from the arrays
// above.  As the animation progresses, the point that each spotlight is
// shining towards will move from pos0 to pos1.
define spot_pos0 pos0[0] + increment * (pos1[0] - pos0[0])
define spot_pos1 pos0[1] + increment * (pos1[1] - pos0[1])
define spot_pos2 pos0[2] + increment * (pos1[2] - pos0[2])

// Place the spotlights
define center0 <-1, 5, -5>
define center1 < 0, 5, -5>
define center2 < 1, 5, -5>

// Define how wide open the spotlight will be, in degrees.
define spot_angle 10

spot_light white, center0, spot_pos0, 1, 0.3 * spot_angle, spot_angle
spot_light white, center1, spot_pos1, 1, 0.3 * spot_angle, spot_angle
spot_light white, center2, spot_pos2, 1, 0.3 * spot_angle, spot_angle
```

continued on next page

continued from previous page
```
// Back wall
object {
    polygon 4, <-10, 0, 10>, <-10, 10, 10>, < 10, 10, 10>, < 10, 0, 10>
    texture { checker matte_white, matte_black }
    }

// Ground plane
object {
    polygon 4, <-10, 0,-10>, <-10, 0, 10>, < 10, 0, 10>, < 10, 0,-10>
    texture { checker matte_white, matte_black }
    }
```

A sequence of frames from the animation is shown in Figure 4-23. The spotlights can be seen lighting separate parts of the back wall at the beginning of the animation. At the end, all three are pointing at the same point on the floor.

WRAP-UP

Throughout this chapter, we touched on a number of individual tricks that can be incorporated into an animation. We only covered a limited selection of the things that are possible in a 3-D animation. All of the topics we discussed can be extended and modified to create new effects. Your creativity and patience are all that are needed.

Each of the samples previously described is supplied on the disks included with this book. Render each of them and start modifying them. As you become more comfortable with the tools, pouring your creativity into an animation will become easier and easier.

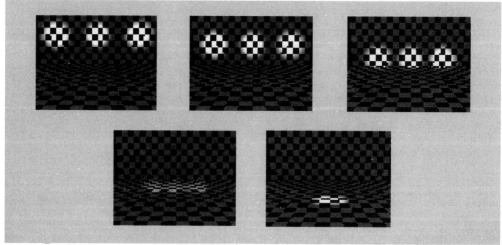

Figure 4-23 Moving Spotlights

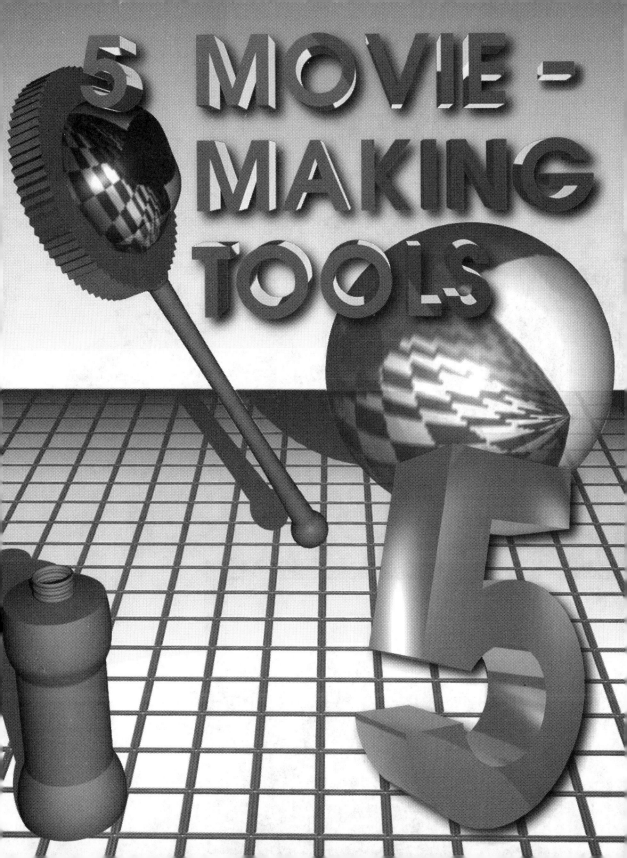

5 MOVIE-MAKING TOOLS

This chapter goes into depth on the capabilities and features of each of the tools included with this book. We'll describe how you can create individual images with Polyray, how to assemble them together into a flic with DTA, and then how to view the flic with Trilobyte Play. When we're done with these three main tools, we'll show you how to generate some additional special effects with SP and DMorf.

POLYRAY

Polyray is a program that converts ASCII data files into rendered images in the Targa format. The rendering capabilities include a wireframe preview display, traditional polygon drawing, and raytracing. Although Polyray does not have the sort of slick graphical user interface (GUI) found in high-end programs, the image quality that can be produced is as good as commercial packages costing thousands of dollars.

After you have written an ASCII data file containing objects, textures, and viewing parameters, Polyray will be able to produce images of your models. Briefly Polyray's capabilities are

- Viewpoint (camera) characteristics
- Light sources, including point, directional (spot), and functional (textured) lights
- Background color
- Surface shading based on standard coloring models, image mapping, or solid texturing
- Many shape primitives: Bezier patch, blob, box, cone, cylinder, disc, implicit function, height field, lathe surface, parabola,

polygon, polynomial function, sphere, extruded surface, torus, and triangular patch

- ◀ Frame-based animation support
- ◀ Conditional processing
- ◀ Include files
- ◀ Named values, objects, and textures
- ◀ Constructive Solid Geometry (CSG)
- ◀ Grids of objects
- ◀ User-definable textures

SHAREWARE INFORMATION

Polyray is a shareware program that may be freely distributed in unmodified form for evaluation purposes. If you use it frequently, you are requested to pay a nominal sum of $35 as a registration fee. For registering you will receive the next version of Polyray free of charge. To register, send the fee to the program's author:

Alexander Enzmann
20 Clinton St.
Woburn, MA 01801
USA

INSTALLATION

Installation instructions for Polyray are contained in Chapter 1, *Introduction*. The rest of this section assumes that the files have been installed in the recommended directory C:\MOVIES\POLYRAY.

SYSTEM REQUIREMENTS

There are two distinct executable files for Polyray included with the book. One requires a 386/387 CPU/FPU combination or a 486DX CPU and the other requires only a 286 CPU. Both versions require at least 2MB of RAM to operate. The 386/387 executable version is the preferred version, as it is smaller, faster, and will be able to use more RAM than the 286 version. Polyray operates in DOS protected mode, due to the large memory requirements during rendering. The size of the program precludes rendering any but the smallest files in real mode DOS.

You need version 3.0 or later of DOS (DR DOS will work also). Polyray will operate with a number of memory managers, including HIMEM and 386MAX. Under Windows 3.0 or later Polyray will operate in a DOS window; however, if you want to use the graphics preview display, you will need to run full screen.

COMMAND LINE OPTIONS

A number of operations can be manipulated through values in an initialization file, within the data file, or from the command line. Command line parameters have the highest precedence, then values in the data file, and last the values in the initialization file. If no arguments are given to Polyray, a list of command line values will be displayed.

The values that can be specified at the command line, with a brief description of their meanings, are listed in Table 5-1.

Table 5-1 ⁘ Polyray's Command Line Switches

Argument	Meaning of Argument
-a	Perform simple antialiasing using neighbor averaging (default: off)
-A	Perform adaptive antialiasing based on threshold (default: off)
-b pixels	Set the maximum number of pixels that will be calculated between file flushes (default: entire file)
-B	Flush the output file every scan line (default: off)
-d probability	Dither objects using the given probabiltiy (default: off)
-D scale	Dither all rays using the given probability (default: off)
-J	Perform jittered antialiasing using a fixed # of samples/pixel (default: off)
-o filename	The output file name, the default output file name if not specified is "out.tga"
-p bits / pixel	Set the number of bits per pixel in the output file. It must be one of 8, 16, 24, 32. (default: 16)

continued on next page

continued from previous page

-P palette	Which palette option to use [0=grey, 1=666, 2=884] (default: 1)
-Q	Abort if any key is hit during trace (default: on)
-q flags	Turn on/off various global shading options (default:63)
-r renderer	Which rendering method: [0=raytrace, 1=scan convert, 2= wireframe] (default: 0)
-R	Resume an interrupted trace (default: off)
-s samples	# of samples per pixel when performing antialiasing (default: 4)
-t status_vals	Status display type [0=none,1=totals,2=line,3=pixel] (default: 2)
-T threshold	Threshold to start oversampling (default: 0.2)
-u	Write the output file in uncompressed form (default: off)
-v	Trace from bottom to top (default: off)
-V mode	Use VGA display while tracing [0=none,1=VGA] (default: 0)
-W	Wait for key before clearing display (default: off)
-x columns	Set the x resolution (default: 256)
-y lines	Set the y resolution (default: 256)
-z start_line	Start a trace at a specified line (default: 0)

None of the command line options need to be specified. Only the input file is required. The simplest command to invoke Polyray would be

```
C:> polyray myfile.pi
```

This will call Polyray with MYFILE.PI as the input. Another example is

```
C:> polyray myfile.pi -x 320 -y 240 -p 8
```

This command will override the resolution statement within MYFILE.PI and will override the default number of bits per pixel in the output Targa image. The output image created by Polyray from this statement will be grayscale with 320x240 pixels.

INITIALIZATION FILE

The first operation carried out by Polyray is to read the initialization file POLYRAY.INI. This file can be used to tune a number of the default variables used during rendering. This file must appear in the current directory. This file does not have to exist, but is typically used as a convenience to eliminate retyping command line parameters.

Each entry in the initialization file must appear on a separate line and have the form:

```
default_name        default_value
```

The names are text. The values are numeric for some names and text for others. The allowed names and values are listed in Table 5-2.

Table 5-2 ♣ Polyray Initialization File Parameters

Default Name	Allowed Values and Keywords
abort_test	true/false/on/off
alias_threshold	[Value to cause adaptive antialiasing to start]
antialias	none/filter/jitter/adaptive
display	none/vga
max_level	[max depth of recursion]
max_lights	[max # of lights]
max_queue_size	[max # of objects in a priority queue]
max_samples	[# samples for jittered/adaptive antialiasing]
pixel_size	[8, 16, 24, 32]
pixel_encoding	none/rle
renderer	ray_trace/scan_convert/wire_frame
shade_flags	[default/bit mask of flags] (see the section on object modifiers for details)
shadow_tolerance	[minimum distance for blocking objects]
status	none/totals/line/pixel

A typical example of POLYRAY.INI would be

```
abort_test          on
alias_threshold     0.05
antialias           adaptive
display             vga
max_samples         8
pixel_size          24
status              line
```

INPUT FILES

An input file describes the basic components of an image:

- ◼◀ A viewpoint that characterizes where the eye is and where it is looking
- ◼◀ Objects, their shape, placement, and orientation
- ◼◀ Light sources, their placement and color

This section of the document describes in detail the syntax of all the components of an input file.

Numeric Expressions

In most places where a number can be used (e.g., scale values, angles, RGB components, etc.) a simple, floating-point expression may be used. The variables a and b are assumed to represent floating-point expressions. The variable V is used to represent a vector expression (see the following table). Numeric expressions can contain any of the terms described in Table 5-3.

Table 5-3 ·•·Polyray Numeric Expressions

Expression	Definition
Value	A floating-point number or defined value (i.e, 1.2, -0.0001, a, b)
(expression)	Parenthesized expression
a ^ b	Exponentiation operator
a * b	Multiplication
a / b	Division

continued on next page

continued from previous page

a + b	Addition
a − b	Subtraction
−x	Unary minus
acos(a)	Arccosine
asin(a)	Arcsin
atan(a)	Arctangent
ceil(a)	Ceiling function
cos(a)	Cosine
cosh(a)	Hyperbolic cosine
degrees(a)	Converts radians to degrees
exp(a)	e^x, standard exponential function
fabs(a)	Absolute value
floor(a)	Floor function
fmod(a, b)	Modulus function for floating-point values
legendre(a, b, c)	Legendre polynomial (l=a,m=b) evaluated at c
ln(a)	Natural logarithm
log(a)	Logarithm base 10
noise(V) noise(V, a)	Turbulence function. The second arg is optional and is the # of octaves.
pow(a, b)	Exponentiation (a^b)
radians(a)	Converts degrees to radians
sin(a)	Sine
sinh(a)	Hyperbolic sine
sqrt(a)	Square root
tan(a)	Tangent
tanh(a)	Hyperbolic tangent
visible(V1, V2)	Returns 1 if second point visible from first.
V[i]	Component i of an array or vector
V1 . V2	Dot product of two vectors
lal	Absolute value (same as fabs)
IVI	Length of a vector

Vector Expressions

In most places where a vector can be used (e.g., color values, rotation angles, locations, ...), a vector expression is allowed. The variables *a*, *b*, and *c* represent floating-point expressions (see Table 5-3). The variables V, V1, and V2 represent vector expressions. Vector expressions can contain any of the terms defined in Table 5-4.

Table 5-4 ⁘Polyray Vector Expressions

Expression	Definition
V1 + V2	Vector addition
V1 - V2	Vector subtraction
V1 * V2	Cross product
V * a a * V	Scaling of a vector by a scalar
V / a	Inverse scaling of a vector by a scalar
brownian(V) dnoise(V)	Makes a random displacement of a vector
dnoise(V, a)	3-D turbulence function. The second arg is optional and is the # of octaves.
color_wheel(a, b, c)	RGB color wheel using a and c (b is ignored), the color returned is based on <a, b> using the following chart:

Where a is the value along the *x*-axis and b is the value along the *z*-axis. Intermediate colors are generated by interpolation.

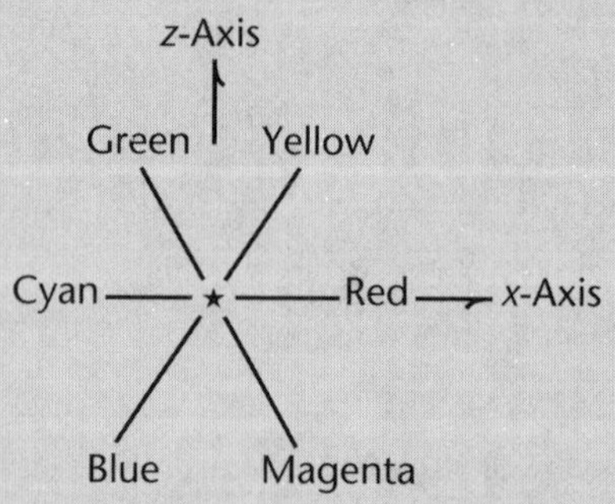

rotate(V1, V2)	Rotate the point specified in the first argument by the angles specified in the second argument (angles in degrees).

continued on next page

Figure 5-1 Tetrahedron

continued from previous page

rotate(V1, V2, a)   Rotate the point V1 about the axis specified by V2. The number of
degrees of rotation is a.

reflect(V1, V2)   Reflect the vector V1 about the vector V2.

Arrays

Arrays are a way to represent data in a convenient list form. A good use for
arrays is to hold a number of locations for polygon vertices or as locations for
objects in successive frames of an animation.

As an example, a way to define a tetrahedron (four-sided Platonic solid) is
to define its vertices, and which vertices make up its faces. Figure 5-1 shows
a diagram of a tetrahedron. By using the vertex and face information in an
object declaration, we can make a tetrahedron out of polygons very easily, as
shown in Listing 5-1.

LISTING 5-1 POLYHDRN.PI
```
define tetrahedron_faces
    [<0, 1, 2>, <0, 2, 3>, <0, 3, 1>, <1, 3, 2>]

define tetrahedron_vertices
    [<0, 0, sqrt(3)>, <0, (2*sqrt(2)*sqrt(3))/3, -sqrt(3)/3>,
     <-sqrt(2), -(sqrt(2)*sqrt(3))/3, -sqrt(3)/3>,
     <sqrt(2), -(sqrt(2)*sqrt(3))/3, -sqrt(3)/3>]
```

continued on next page

continued from previous page

```
define tcf tetrahedron_faces
define tcv tetrahedron_vertices
define tetrahedron
object {
   object { polygon 3, tcv[tcf[ 0][0]], tcv[tcf[ 0][1]], tcv[tcf[ 0][2]] } +
   object { polygon 3, tcv[tcf[ 1][0]], tcv[tcf[ 1][1]], tcv[tcf[ 1][2]] } +
   object { polygon 3, tcv[tcf[ 2][0]], tcv[tcf[ 2][1]], tcv[tcf[ 2][2]] } +
   object { polygon 3, tcv[tcf[ 3][0]], tcv[tcf[ 3][1]], tcv[tcf[ 3][2]] }
   }
```

In the object declaration, each polygon grabbed a series of vertex indices from the array tetrahedron_faces, then used that index to grab the actual location in space of that vertex.

Another example is to use an array to store a series of view directions so that we can use animation to generate a series of very distinct renders of the same scene. See the section on functional textures at the end of this chapter for an example of how that technique is used to build an environment map.

Definition of the Viewpoint

The viewpoint and its associated components define the position and orientation from which the view will be generated. The format of the declaration is

```
viewpoint {
   from vexper
   at vexper
   up vexper
   angle fexper
   resolution fexper, fexper
   aspect fexper
   hither fexper
   yon fexper
   dither_rays fexper
   dither_objects fexper
   max_trace_depth fexper
   aperture fexper
   focal_distance fexper
   }
```

The order of the entries defining the viewpoint is not important, unless you redefine some field. (In that case the definition farthest down the list is used.) The meaning of each entry and the default value are shown in Table 5-5. The first six entries (aspect ... from) are the most important because they set the orientation of the camera and the layout of the image file. The remaining entries are used for special effects.

Table 5-5 ⊹ Polyray Viewpoint Statements

Statement	Definition
aspect	The ratio of width to height (Default: 1.0)
at	A position to be at the center of the image, in XYZ world coordinates. (Default: <0, 0, 0>)
angle	The field of view (in degrees), from the center of the top row to the center of the bottom row. (Default: 45 degrees)
from	The eye location in XYZ. (Default: <0, 0, -10>)
resolution	The number of pixels wide and high of the raster. (Default: 256x256)
up	A vector defining which direction is up, as an XYZ vector. (Default: <0, 1, 0>)
hither	Distance to front of view pyramid. Any intersection less than this value will be ignored. (Default: 1.0e-3)
yon	Distance to back of view pyramid. Any intersection beyond this distance will be ignored. (Default: 1.0e5)
dither_rays	Rays will be skipped if a random number is above the given value.
dither_objects	For each ray, Ray-surface checks will skipped for an object if a random number is above the given value.
max_trace_depth	This allows you to tailor the amount of recursion allowed for scenes with reflection and/or transparency. (Default: 5)
aperture	If larger than 0, then extra rays are shot (controlled by max_samples in the initialization file) to produce a blurred image. (Good values are between 0.1 and 0.5.)
focal_distance	Distance from the eye to the point that things are in focus, this defaults to the distance between from and at.

An example of a simple viewpoint declaration that puts the eye behind and above the origin, and looking at the origin, would be

```
viewpoint {
   from <0, 5, -10>
   at <0, 0, 0>
   up <0, 1, 0>
   }
```

Object Modifiers

The position, orientation, and size of an object can be modified through one of four linear transformations: translation, rotation, scaling, and shear. The shading options for a particular object are controlled by the shading flags statement.

TRANSLATION

Translation moves the position of an object by the number of units specified in the associated vector. The format of the declaration is

```
translate <xt, yt, zt>
```

ROTATION

Rotation revolves the position of an object about the x-, y-, and z-axes (in that order). The amount of rotation is specified in degrees for each of the axes. The direction of rotation follows a left-handed convention. If the thumb of your left hand points along the positive direction of an axis, then the direction your fingers curl is the positive direction of rotation.

The format of the declaration is

```
rotate <xr, yr, zr>
```

For example, the declaration

```
rotate <30, 0, 20>
```

will rotate the object by 30 degrees about the x-axis, followed by 20 degrees about the z-axis. Remember: Left-Handed Rotations.

SCALING

Scaling alters the size of an object by a given amount with respect to each of the coordinate axes. The format of the declaration is

```
scale <xs, ys, zs>
```

Figure 5-2 Linear Shear

SHEAR

An occasionally useful transformation is linear shear. Shear scales along one axis by an amount that is proportional to the location on another axis. The format of the declaration is

```
shear yx, zx, xy, zy, xz, yz
```

Typically, only one or two of the components will be nonzero. For example, the declaration

```
shear 0, 0, 1, 0, 0, 0
```

will shear an object more and more to the right as y gets larger and larger. The order of the letters in the declaration is descriptive. For example, shear ... ab, ... means shear along direction a by the amount "ab" times the position b. Figure 5-2 shows the effect of shear in the x-axis. If you were looking directly along the z-axis, then that figure would correspond to the previous shear declaration.

SHADING FLAGS

It is possible to tune the shading that will be performed for each object. The values of each bit in the flag have the meanings shown in Table 5-6.

The declaration has the following form, where **xx** is the sum of the individual shading flags. The default is 32+16+8+4+2+1, or 63.

```
shading_flags xx
```

The flag for primary rays (value 32) should only be turned off to create special effects. As an example of using these flags, suppose we want an object to be reflective and to be able to cast shadows. The shading flags for that object would be

32	To make it visible
16	So it will cast shadows
2	So reflections will be checked

The resulting declaration is written as

```
shading_flags 32+16+2
```

Note: The shading flag only affects the object in which the declaration is made. This means that if you want the shading values affected for all parts of an aggregate object, you will need a declaration in every component.

Table 5-6 ⚬ Zooming Into a Scene

Flag	Name	Meaning
1	Shadow_Check	Shadows will be generated on this object.
2	Reflection_Check	Reflection will be checked for this object.
4	Transmission_Check	Transparency will be checked for this object.
8	Two_Sides	If set, highlighting will be performed for both sides of this object.
16	Cast_Shadow	This object can cast shadows.
32	Primary_Rays	If off, then primary rays (those from the eye) will not be checked against this object.

Primitives

Primitives are the lowest level of shape description. Typically, a scene will contain many primitives, appearing either individually or as aggregates using either Constructive Solid Geometry (CSG) operations or gridded objects.

The primitive shapes that can be used in Polyray include the following:

- Bezier patch
- Blob
- Box
- Cone
- Cylinder
- Disk
- Implicit surface
- Height field
- Lathe surface
- Parabola
- Polygon
- Polynomial surface
- Sphere
- Sweep surface
- Torus
- Triangular patch

Descriptions and brief examples are given of each of these primitive shapes. Following the descriptions of the primitives are descriptions of how CSG objects and grids can be built.

BEZIER PATCHES

A Bezier patch is a form of spline patch that interpolates a 4x4 array of control vertices. The patch declaration has several tuning values followed by the array of control vertices. The format of the declaration is

```
bezier subdivision_type, flatness_value,
       u_subdivisions, v_subdivision,
       [ 16 comma-separated vertices, i.e.
       <x0, y0, z0>, <x1, y1, z1>, ..., <x15, y15, z15> ]
```

The value of `subdivision_type` controls how the patch is represented internally. The valid values and their meaning are

- For this type, Polyray will store only the minimum information needed to render the patch. The advantage is that only enough RAM is needed to describe the surface. The disadvantage is that raytracing is slow.

- For this type, Polyray stores a hierarchical tree of bounding spheres that contain smaller and smaller pieces of the patch. This tree is used during rendering to speed up the ray-surface intersection process. Raytracing will be faster, but it can require much more memory.

`flatness_value` is used to determine how far a patch should be subdivided before it is considered flat enough. The smaller this value, the more the patch will be subdivided (limited by the next two values).

The number of levels of subdivision of the patch, in each direction, is controlled by the two parameters `u_subdivisions` and `v_subdivisions`. The more subdivisions allowed, the smoother the approximation to the patch; however, storage space and processing time increase.

An example of a Bezier patch is shown in the following code. Figure 5-3 shows the result of rendering this patch.

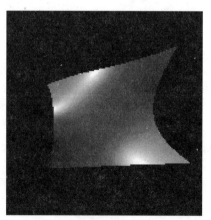

Figure 5-3 Single Bezier Patch

```
object {
  bezier 2, 0.05, 3, 3,
    < 0, 0, 2>, < 1, 0, 0>, < 2, 0, 0>, < 3, 0,-2>,
    < 0, 1, 0>, < 1, 1, 0>, < 2, 1, 0>, < 3, 1, 0>,
    < 0, 2, 0>, < 1, 2, 0>, < 2, 2, 0>, < 3, 2, 0>,
    < 0, 3, 2>, < 1, 3, 0>, < 2, 3, 0>, < 3, 3,-2>
  translate <-1.5, -1.5, 0>
  scale <2, 2, 2>
  rotate <10, -20, 0>
  shiny_red
}
```

Figure 5-4 shows a classical computer graphics model, a teapot composed of 32 Bezier patches. The data for this graphics image is included with the Polyray data files.

BLOB

A blob describes a smooth potential field around one or more spherical, cylindrical, or planar components. Blobs are useful for modeling organic or liquid shapes. When components of a blob are near each other, the blob surface flows smoothly from one component to another. The format of the declaration is

```
blob threshold:
    blob_component1
    [, blob_component2 ]
    [, etc. for each component ]
```

Figure 5-4 Teapot Made from 32 Bezier Patches

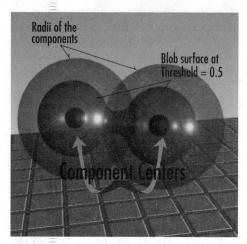

Figure 5-5 Schematic of Addition of
Blob Components

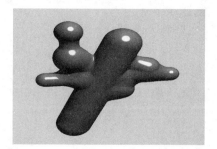

Figure 5-6 Sample Blob Shape

The threshold is the minimum potential value that will be considered when examining the interaction of the various components of the blob. Each blob component may appear in one of three forms:

```
sphere <x, y, z>, strength, radius
cylinder <x0, y0, z0>, <x1, y1, z1>, strength, radius
plane <nx, ny, nz>, d, strength, dist
```

The strength component describes how strong the potential field is around the center of the component. The radius component describes the maximum distance at which the component will interact with other components. For a spherical blob component, the vector <x,y,z> gives the center of the potential field around the component. For a cylindrical blob component, the vector <x0, y0, z0> defines one end of the axis of a cylinder, and the vector <x1, y1, z1> defines the other end of the axis of a cylinder. A planar blob component is defined by the standard plane equation with <nx, ny, nz> defining the normal, and d defines the distance of the plane from the origin along the normal.

Figure 5-5 diagrams the interaction of two spherical blob components. The radius of each component is shown as a dashed circle. The centers of the components are the heavy dots. In the diagram, it is assumed that the strength of each component is 1. The surface that is formed for a threshold value of 0.5 is indicated by the heavy curves. If threshold is lowered, the surface of the blob will move outward toward the dashed circles. If threshold is raised, then the surface will move inward toward the component centers, first separating into two pieces and then, as threshold goes above 1, the blob will vanish.

Listing 5-1 is an example of a blob declaration. The image of that blob is shown in Figure 5-6. This particular blob combines cylindrical and spherical components.

```
object {
   blob 0.5:
      cylinder <0,  0, 0>, <5, 0, 0>, 1, 0.7,
      cylinder <1, -3, 0>, <3, 2, 0>, 1, 1.4,
      sphere <3, -0.8, 0>, 1, 1,
      sphere <4,  0.5, 0>, 1, 1,
      sphere <1,  1,   0>, 1, 1,
      sphere <1,  1.5, 0>, 1, 1,
      sphere <1,  2.7, 0>, 1, 1
   shiny_red
   }
```

BOX

A box is a rectangular solid that has its edges aligned with the x-, y-, and z-axes. It is defined in terms of two diagonally opposite corners. The alignment can be changed by rotations after the shape declaration. The format of the declaration is

```
box <x0, y0, z0>, <x1, y1, z1>
```

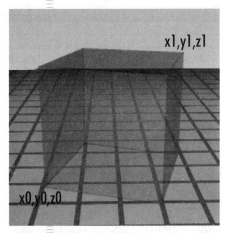

Figure 5-7 Schematic of a Box

Figure 5-8 Stacked Boxes

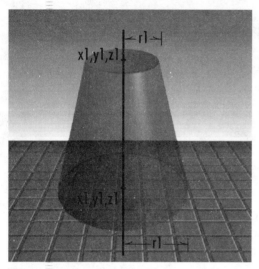

Figure 5-9 Schematic of a Cone

Figure 5-10 Cone

The convention is that the first point is the front, lower-left point and the second is the back, upper-right point. Figure 5-7 shows a diagram of a box with the corners labeled.

Listing 5-2 stacks four boxes on top of each other. Figure 5-8 shows a rendered image of the boxes.

LISTING 5-2 STACKING BOXES
```
object {
      object { box <-1, 3, -1>, <1, 4, 1> }
    + object { box <-2, 2, -2>, <2, 3, 2> }
    + object { box <-3, 1, -3>, <3, 2, 3> }
    + object { box <-4, 0, -4>, <4, 1, 4> }
    matte_blue
    }
```

CONE

A cone is defined in terms of a base point, an apex point, and the radii at those two points. Cones are not closed. A schematic of a cone primitive is shown in Figure 5-9. The format of the declaration is

```
cone <x0, y0, z0>, r0, <x1, y1, z1>, r1
```

A cone is declared in Listing 5-3. The rendered image of that cone is shown in Figure 5-10.

LISTING 5-3 A CONE
```
object {
   cone <0, 0, 0>, 2, <0, 4, 0>, 0
   shiny_red
   }
```

CYLINDER

A cylinder is defined in terms of a bottom point, a top point, and its radius. Note that cylinders are not closed. Figure 5-11 diagrams a cylinder. The format of the declaration is

```
cylinder <x0, y0, z0>, <x1, y1, z1>, r
```

The code in Listing 5-4 creates a cylinder. A rendered image of the cylinder is shown in Figure 5-12.

LISTING 5-4 A CYLINDER
```
object {
      cylinder <0, -2, 0>, <0, 2, 0>, 2
      shiny_red
      }
```

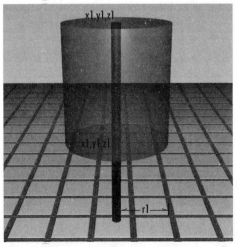

Figure 5-11 Schematic of a Cylinder

Figure 5-12 Cylinder

DISK

A disk is defined in terms of a center, a normal, an optional inner radius, and an outer radius. If only one radius is given, then the disk has the appearance of a (very) flat coin. If two radii are given, then the disk takes the shape of an annulus (washer) where the disk extends from the first radius to the second radius. Typical uses for disks are as caps for cones and cylinders, or as ground planes (using really big radii). The format of the declaration is one of the following:

```
disc <cx, cy, cz>, <nx, ny, nz>, r
disc <cx, cy, cz>, <nx, ny, nz>, ir, or
```

The center vector `<cx,cy,cz>` defines where the center of the disk is located, the normal vector `<nx,ny,nz>` defines the direction that is perpendicular to the disk (i.e., a disc having the center <0,0,0> and the normal <0,1,0> would put the disk in the x-z plane with the *y*-axis coming straight out of the center). A schematic of a disk primitive is shown in Figure 5-13.

An example of a disk is shown in Listing 5-5. The rendered image of that disk is shown in Figure 5-14.

LISTING 5-5 A DISK
```
object {
    disc <0, 2, 0>, <0, 1, 0>, 1, 3
    rotate <-30, 20, 0>
    blue_ripple { scale <0.2, 0.2, 0.2> }
    }
```

Note: A disk is infinitely thin. If you look at it edge-on it will disappear.

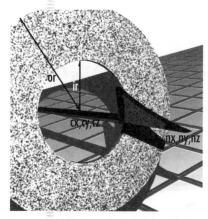

Figure 5-13 Schematic of a Disk

Figure 5-14 Disk with a Ripple Texture

IMPLICIT SURFACE

An implicit surface is used for a general function of the variables *x*, *y*, and *z*. This declaration allows a wide class of surfaces to be defined and rendered. The format of the declaration is

```
function f(x,y,z)
```

The function f(x,y,z) may be any algebraic expression composed of the variables *x*, *y*, *z*; a numerical value (e.g., 0.5); the operators +, -, *, /, ^; and the functions cos, cosh, exp, fabs, ln, log, sin, sinh, tan, and tanh. The code is not particularly fast, nor is it totally accurate; however, the capability to raytrace such a wide class of functions by a shareware program is (We believe) unique to Polyray. See the Polyray documentation for further details.

As an example of an implicit surface, Listing 5-6 defines a form of a superquadric surface. The result of rendering this surface is shown in Figure 5-15.

LISTING 5-6 A SUPERQUADRIC SURFACE

```
// Define a superquadric surface
object {
    function |x|^0.75 + |y|^0.74 + |z|^0.75 - 1
    shiny_red
    bounding_box <-1, -1, -1>, <1, 1, 1>
    u_steps 40
    v_steps 40
    rotate <0, 30, 0>
    }
```

Figure 5-15 Superquadric Pinchy

HEIGHT FIELD

A height field is a way of representing single value functions (altitudes) over a rectangular mesh. Height fields are a very efficient way of representing terrains or certain forms of mathematical surfaces.

Polyray supports two ways to create height fields. They can be generated using data stored in a data file (which must have a specific format) or using an implicit function of the form y = f(x, z).

The default orientation of a height field is that the entire field lies in the square 0 <= x <= 1, 0 <= z <= 1. File-based height fields are always in this orientation. Implicit height fields can optionally be defined over a different area of the x-z plane. The height value is used for *y*. See the Polyray document archives for further information on using height fields.

The format of a file-based height field is one of the following:

```
height_field "filename"
smooth_height_field "filename"
```

The format of an implicit height field is one of the following:

```
height_fn xsize, zsize, min_x, max_x, min_z, max_z, expression
height_fn xsize, zsize, expression
smooth_height_fn xsize, zsize, min_x, max_x, min_z, max_z, expression
smooth_height_fn xsize, zsize, expression
```

If the four values min_x, max_x, min_z, and max_z are not defined, the default square 0 <= x <= 1, 0 <= z <= 1 will be used.

For example, Listing 5-7 builds a height field by evaluating the noise function over a grid. Four octaves are used in noise to create the various levels of bumpiness. In the listing below, the variable P is generated automatically as the height function is evaluated. P takes the value of each of the points <x, 0, z> within the height field mesh. The mesh is defined to have 256 distinct x values from –4 to 4, and 256 distinct z values from –4 to 4. The rendered image of this object is shown in Figure 5-16.

LISTING 5-7 AN IMPLICIT FIELD
```
// Define a noise based height field
object {
   height_fn 256, 256, -4, 4, -4, 4, 1.5 * (noise(P, 4) - 0.5)
   shiny_white
   }
```

Figure 5-16 Height Field Landscape

A number of examples of creating height fields, both file based and implicit, are included with the Polyray documents.

LATHE SURFACES

A lathe surface is a polygon that has been revolved about the y-axis. This surface allows you to build objects that are symmetric about an axis, simply by defining 2-D points.

The format of the declaration is

```
lathe type, direction, total_vertices,
    <vert1.x,vert1.y,vert1.z>
    [, <vert2.x, vert2.y, vert2.z>]
    [, etc. for total_vertices vertices]
```

The value of type is either 1 or 2. If the value is 1, the surface will simply revolve the line segments. If the value is 2, the surface will be represented by a spline that approximates the line segments that were given. A lathe surface of type 2 is a very good way to smooth off corners in a set of line segments.

The value of the vector direction is used to change the orientation of the lathe. For a lathe surface that is straight up and down the y-axis, use <0,1,0> for direction. For a lathe surface that lies on the x-axis, you would use <1,0,0> for direction.

Note that Constructive Solid Geometry (CSG) will work correctly only when you close the lathe—either make the end point of the lathe the same as the start point, or make the x-value of the start and end points equal zero. Lathes, unlike polygons, are not automatically closed by Polyray.

Figure 5-17 Lathe Surface with a Portion Cut Away

An example of a lathe object is provided in Listing 5-8. Note that a piece of the lathe is cut away by a box. A rendered image of this lathe is shown in Figure 5-17.

LISTING 5-8 A LATHE

```
define lathe_object
object {
    lathe 2, <0, 1, 0>, 12,
        <2, -1>, <3, -1>, <3.4, -2>, <4, -1.1>, <3.6, -0.9>,
        <2.6, 0>,
        <3.6, 0.9>, <4, 1.1>, <3.4, 2>, <3, 1>, <2, 1>,
        <2, -1>
    }

object {
    lathe_object { shiny_red }
    - object { box <0, -5, 0>, <5, 5, -5> shiny_green }
    rotate <0, 30, 0>
    }
```

PARABOLA

A parabola is a quadratic surface that resembles the end of an egg, or perhaps a salt shaker. A parabola is defined in terms of a bottom point, a top point, and its radius at the bottom. A schematic of the parabola primitive is shown in Figure 5-18. The format of the declaration is

```
parabola <x0, y0, z0>, <x1, y1, z1>, r
```

The vector <x0, y0, z0> defines the top of the parabola. The top being the part that comes to a point. The vector <x1, y1, z1> defines the bottom of the parabola. The width of the parabola at the bottom is r.

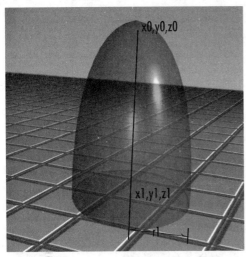

Figure 5-19 Parabola

Figure 5-18 Schematic of a Parabola

An example of a parabola declaration is shown in Listing 5-9. A rendered image of that parabola is shown in Figure 5-19.

LISTING 5-9 A PARABOLA

```
object {
   parabola <0, 6, 0>, <0, -1, 0>, 2
   shiny_red
   }
```

POLYGON

Although polygons are not very interesting mathematically, there are many sorts of objects that are easy to represent with polygons. Polyray assumes that all polygons are closed and automatically adds a side from the last vertex to the first vertex.

The format of the declaration is

```
polygon total_vertices,
   <v1.x,v1.y,v1.z>
   [, <v2.x, v2.y, v2.z>]
   [, etc. for total_vertices vertices]
```

As with the sphere, note the comma separating each vertex of the polygon. A diagram showing the outline of a polygon is shown in Figure 5-20. Note that the polygon may have indentations.

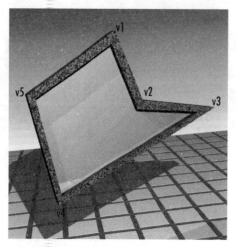

Figure 5-20 Outline of a Polygon

Figure 5-21 Polygon

Polygons are used as floors in a lot of images. They are a little slower than the corresponding plane, but for scan conversion they are a lot easier to handle. An example of a checkered floor made from a polygon is shown in Listing 5-10. A rendered image is shown in Figure 5-21.

LISTING 5-10 A CHECKERED FLOOR

```
object {
    polygon 5, <-5, 0, -2>, <-5, 0, 5>, <0, 0, 2>,
            <5, 0, 5>, <5, 0, -2>
    texture {
      checker shiny_red, shiny_blue
      scale <2, 1, 2>
      }
    }
```

POLYNOMIAL SURFACE

A polynomial surface is an implicit surface that is limited to positive, whole powers of x, y, and z. Examples of polynomial surfaces include cones, cylinders, and parabolas. The Polyray data files include a number of examples of

Figure 5-22 Polynomial Surface

polynomial surfaces that exhibit a wide variety of shapes. The format of the declaration is

```
polynomial f(x,y,z)
```

The function f(x,y,z) must be a simple polynomial (i.e., $x^2+y^2+z^2-1.0$ is the definition of a sphere of radius 1 centered at (0,0,0)). See the Polyray documents for further details on polynomial surfaces.

Listing 5-11 creates a polynomial surface of order 6. The surface itself is shown in Figure 5-22.

LISTING 5-11 A POLYNOMIAL SURFACE

```
define a 1
define c 2
object {
    polynomial y^2 + z^2 - c^2*a^2*x^4 + c^2*x^6
    bounding_box <-1, -1, -1>, <1, 1, 1>
    rotate <0, -30, 0>
    shiny_red
    }
```

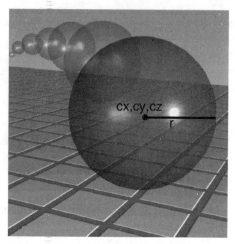

Figure 5-23 Schematic of a Sphere

SPHERES

Spheres are the simplest 3-D objects to render and a sphere primitive enjoys a speed advantage over most other primitives. A schematic of a sphere is shown in Figure 5-23. The format of the declaration is

```
sphere <cx, cy, cz>, r
```

A basic benchmark file is a single sphere illuminated by a single light, as shown in Listing 5-12. A rendered image of the sphere is shown in Figure 5-24.

LISTING 5-12 AN ILLUMINATED SPHERE
```
object {
  sphere <0, 0, 0>, 2
  shiny_red
  }
```

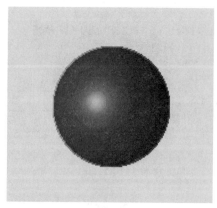

Figure 5-24 Sphere

SWEEP SURFACE

A sweep surface, also referred to as an extruded surface, is a polygon that has been swept along a given direction. It can be used to make multisided beams, or to create ribbon-like objects.

The format of the declaration is

```
sweep type, direction, total_vertices,
  <vert1.x,vert1.y,vert1.z>
  [, <vert2.x, vert2.y, vert2.z>]
  [, etc. for total_vertices vertices]
```

The value of `type` may be either 1 or 2. If the value is 1, the surface will be a set of connected squares. If the value is 2, the surface will be represented by a spline that approximates the line segments that were given.

The value of the vector `direction` is used to change the orientation of the sweep. For a sweep surface that is extruded straight up and down the *y*-axis, use <0, 1, 0> for `direction`. The size of the vector `direction` will also affect the amount of extrusion, (i.e., if |direction|= 2, then the extrusion will be two units in that direction). Figure 5-25 shows a star shape extruded as a sweep surface.

An example of a sweep surface is provided in Listing 5-13. This example uses exactly the same data points as the example used for the lathe surface. A comparison of the two images demonstrates the similarities and differences between lathe and sweep surfaces. The rendered image is shown in Figure 5-26.

Figure 5-25 Extruded Star

Figure 5-26 Sweep Surface

107

LISTING 5-13 A SWEEP SURFACE

```
define sweep_object
object {
    sweep 2, <0, 1, 0>, 12,
        <2, -1>, <3, -1>, <3.4, -2>, <4, -1.1>, <3.6, -0.9>,
        <2.6, 0>,
        <3.6, 0.9>, <4, 1.1>, <3.4, 2>, <3, 1>, <2, 1>,
        <2, -1>
    u_steps 16
    shiny_red
    }

object {
    sweep_object
    * object { box <-5, 0, -5>, <5, 1, 5> shiny_green }
    }
```

Note that CSG will work correctly only if you close the sweep—make the end point of the sweep the same as the start point. Sweeps, unlike polygons, are not automatically closed by Polyray.

TORUS

The torus primitive is a doughnut-shaped surface that is defined by a center point, the distance from the center point to the middle of the ring of the doughnut, the radius of the ring of the doughnut, and the orientation of the surface. A schematic of a torus is shown in Figure 5-27.

The format of the declaration is

```
torus r0, r1, <cx, cy, cz>, <nx, ny, nz>
```

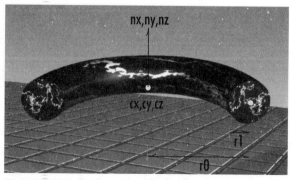

Figure 5-27 Schematic of a Torus

As an example, a torus that has major radius 1, has minor radius 0.4, and is oriented so that the ring lies in the x-z plane is listed in the following code (Listing 5-14). A rendered image of the torus is shown in Figure 5-28.

LISTING 5-14 A TORUS

```
object {
   torus 1, 0.4, <0, 0, 0>, <0, 1, 0>
   shiny_red
   }
```

TRIANGULAR PATCHES

A triangular patch is defined by a set of vertices and their normals. When calculating shading information for a triangular patch, the normal information is used to interpolate the final normal from the intersection point to produce a smooth, shaded triangle. A schematic of a triangle patch is shown in Figure 5-29.

The format of the declaration is

```
patch <v1.x,v1.y,v1.z>, <n1.x,n1.y,n1.z>,
      <v2.x,v2.y,v2.z>, <n2.x,n2.y,n2.z>,
      <v3.x,v3.y,v3.z>, <n3.x,n3.y,n3.z>
```

CONSTRUCTIVE SOLID GEOMETRY (CSG)

Constructive Solid Geometry (CSG) is a very compact way to build up new objects. By using CSG, it is possible to collect several objects into a single one,

Figure 5-29 Schematic of a Triangle Patch

Figure 5-28 Torus

making it possible to manipulate the collection as a unit. CSG operations also provide a way to create objects that can't be described as a simple collection. By using intersection or difference operations, it is possible to drill holes or carve ridges into an object.

CSG objects in Polyray can be defined in terms of the union, intersection, and inverse of other objects. Unions are a way to collect objects together. Intersections are the way to use one object to carve a piece out of another object. The inverse operation is used to reverse the inside and outside of an object. The CSG operations allowed in Polyray and the format of their declarations are listed as follows.

```
csgexper + csgexper   - Union
csgexper * csgexper   - Intersection
csgexper - csgexper   - Difference
csgexper & csgexper   - Clip the first object by the second
~csgexper             - Inverse
(csgexper)            - Parenthesised expression
```

Figure 5-30 shows the union, intersection, difference, and clipping operations using a sphere and a box. These operations are arranged left to right, top to bottom.

Union operations are the easiest with which to work. All pieces of all objects in a union will be rendered. There are no restrictions or unusual difficulties that will arise from adding two or more objects together with a CSG union.

Intersection and difference require that the objects involved have a clear inside and outside. In an intersection, only those pieces of each surface that

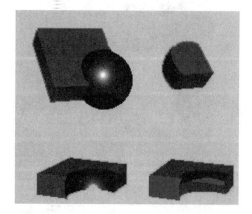

Figure 5-30 Union, Intersection, Difference, and Clipping

are inside both objects will be rendered. The difference operation is the same as the intersection of an object with the inverse of another object. In other words, in a CSG difference operation, the pieces of the surfaces that are kept are those that are inside the first object and outside the second object.

Not all Polyray primitives have well-defined sides. Those that do include spheres, boxes, polynomials, blobs, and functions. Surfaces that do not always have a clear inside/outside, but work reasonably well in CSG intersections, include cylinders, cones, disks, lathes, parabolas, polygons, and sweeps.

Some care must be taken when using cylinders, cones, and parabolas in CSG operations. The open ends of these surfaces will also be open in the resulting CSG. To close them off, you can use a disk primitive positioned at the open ends.

Using disks and polygons in a CSG is really the same as doing a CSG with the plane in which they lie. If fact, a disk is an excellent choice for clipping or intersecting an object, as the inside/outside test is very fast.

Lathes and sweeps use Jordan's rule to determine if a point is inside. This means that given a test point, if a line from that point to infinity crosses the surface an odd number of times, then the point is inside. The net result is that if the lathe (or sweep) is not closed, then you may get unexpected results in a CSG intersection (or difference).

As an example, the following listing (Listing 5-15) builds an object made up of a sphere of radius 1 with a hole of radius 0.5 through the middle. The rendered image is shown in Figure 5-31.

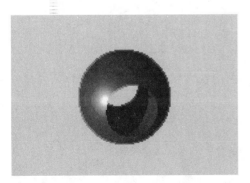

Figure 5-31 Subtracting a Cylinder from a Sphere Using CSG

LISTING 5-15 SPHERE WITH A HOLE

```
define cylinder_z object { cylinder <0, 0, -5>, <0, 0, 5>, 0.5 }
define unit_sphere object { sphere <0, 0, 0>, 1 }

// Define a CSG shape by deleting a cylinder from a sphere
object {
    unit_sphere - cylinder_z
    shiny_red
    }
```

GRIDDED OBJECTS

A gridded object is a way to compactly represent a rectangular arrangement of objects by using an image map. Each object is placed within a 1x1 cube that has its lower-left corner at the location $<i, 0, j>$ and its upper-right corner at $<i+1,1,j+1>$. The color index of each pixel in the image map is used to determine which of a set of objects will be placed at the corresponding position in space.

The gridded object is much faster to render than the corresponding layout of objects. The major drawback is that every object must be scaled and translated to completely fit into a 1x1x1 cube that has corners at <0,0,0> and <1,1,1>.

The size of the entire grid is determined by the number of pixels in the image. A 16x32 image would go from 0 to 16 along the x-axis, and the last row would range from 0 to 16 at 31 units in z out from the x-axis.

The format of the declaration is

```
gridded "image.tga",
    object1
    object2
    object3
    ...
```

Listing 5-16 is an example of how a gridded object is declared:

LISTING 5-16 A GRIDDED OBJECT

```
define tiny_sphere object { sphere <0.5, 0.4, 0.5>, 0.4 }
define pointy_cone object { cone <0.5, 0.5, 0.5>, 0.4, <0.5, 1, 0.5>, 0 }

object {
    gridded "grdimg0.tga",
        tiny_sphere { shiny_coral }
        tiny_sphere { shiny_red }
        pointy_cone { shiny_green }
    translate <-10, 0, -10>
    rotate <0, 210, 0>
    }
```

Figure 5-32
16 x 16 Image Used for a
Gridded Object

In the image GRDIMG0.TGA, there are a total of three colors used. Every pixel that uses color index 0 will generate a shiny, coral-colored sphere. Every pixel that uses index will generate a red sphere. Every pixel that uses index 2 will generate a green cone. And every other color index used in the image will leave the corresponding space empty. GRDIMG0.TGA is shown in Figure 5-32. The gridded object defined in the previous code is shown in Figure 5-33.

Several examples using grids of objects are included in the Polyray data file.

Color and Lighting

The color space used in Polyray is RGB. Colors are represented as a set of intensities of the primary colors: red, green, and blue. The values of each component must be in the range 0 -> 1. The way the color and shading of surfaces is specified is described in the following sections.

In Polyray, RGB colors may be defined as either a three-component vector or a named color. A color vector would have a form like <0.6, 0.196078, 0.8> with the components defining the intensities of red, green, and blue respectively, or as one of a number of named colors such as `DarkOrchid`. Table 5-7 gives the values associated with each of the predefined colors available in Polyray.

Figure 5-33 Gridded Object Composed
of Spheres and Cones

Table 5-7 ❖ Predefined Colors

Color	Red Value	Green Value	Blue Value
Aquamarine	.439216	.858824	.576471
Black	0	0	0
Blue	0	0	1
BlueViolet	.623529	.372549	.623529
Brown	.647059	.164706	.164706
CadetBlue	.372549	.623529	.623529
Coral	1	.498039	0
CornflowerBlue	.258824	.258824	.435294
Cyan	0	1	1
DarkGreen	.184314	.309804	.184314
DarkOliveGreen	.309804	.309804	.184314
DarkOrchid	.6	.196078	.8
DarkSlateBlue	.419608	.137255	.556863
DarkSlateGray	.184314	.309804	.309804
DarkSlateGrey	.184314	.309804	.309804
DarkTurquoise	.439216	.576471	.858824
DimGray	.329412	.329412	.329412
DimGrey	.329412	.329412	.329412
Firebrick	.556863	.137255	.137255
ForestGreen	.137255	.556863	.137255
Gold	.8	.498039	.196078
Goldenrod	.858824	.858824	.439216
Gray	.752941	.752941	.752941
Green	0	1	0
GreenYellow	.576471	.858824	.439216
Grey	.752941	.752941	.752941
IndianRed	.309804	.184314	.184314
Khaki	.623529	.623529	.372549
LightBlue	.74902	.847059	.847059
LightGray	.658824	.658824	.658824

Continued on next page

Continued from previous page

LightGrey	.658824	.658824	.658824
LightSteelBlue	.560784	.560784	.737255
LimeGreen	.196078	.8	.196078
Magenta	1	0	1
Maroon	.556863	.137255	.419608
MediumAquamarine	.196078	.8	.6
MediumBlue	.196078	.196078	.8
MediumForestGreen	.419608	.556863	.137255
MediumGoldenrod	.917647	.917647	.678431
MediumOrchid	.576471	.439216	.858824
MediumSeaGreen	.258824	.435294	.258824
MediumSlateBlue	.498039	0	1
MediumSpringGreen	.498039	1	0
MediumTurquoise	.439216	.858824	.858824
MediumVioletRed	.858824	.439216	.576471
MidnightBlue	.184314	.184314	.309804
Navy	.137255	.137255	.556863
NavyBlue	.137255	.137255	.556863
Orange	.8	.196078	.196078
OrangeRed	1	0	.498039
Orchid	.858824	.439216	.858824
PaleGreen	.560784	.737255	.560784
Pink	.737255	.560784	.560784
Plum	.917647	.678431	.917647
Red	1	0	0
Salmon	.435294	.258824	.258824
SeaGreen	.137255	.556863	.419608
Sienna	.556863	.419608	.137255
SkyBlue	.196078	.6	.8
SlateBlue	0	.498039	1
SpringGreen	0	1	.498039
SteelBlue	.137255	.419608	.556863

Continued on next page

Continued from previous page

Tan	.858824	.576471	.439216
Thistle	.847059	.74902	.847059
Turquoise	.678431	.917647	.917647
Violet	.309804	.184314	.309804
VioletRed	.8	.196078	.6
Wheat	.847059	.847059	.74902
White	.988235	.988235	.988235
Yellow	1	1	0
YellowGreen	.6	.8	.196078

The coloring of objects is determined by the interaction of lights, the shape of the surface they are striking, and the characteristics of the surface itself.

Light Sources

Light sources may be simple positional light sources, spotlights, or textured lights. None of these lights has any physical size. The lights do not appear in the scene, only the effects of the lights.

POSITIONAL LIGHTS

A positional light is defined by its RGB color and its <x,y,z> position. The format of the declaration is one of these:

```
light color, location
light location
```

White is the default color, so the second declaration will use white as the color of the light.

SPOT LIGHTS

Spotlights generate light only within a cone. In addition to being able to alter the color of the light, you can alter the width of the cone-shaped beam and the edges of the spot of light that is cast with spotlights. The format of the declaration is

```
spot_light color, location, pointed_at, Tightness, Angle, Falloff
spot_light location, pointed_at
```

The vector location defines the position of the spotlight. The vector pointed_at defines the point at which the spotlight is directed. The optional components are

- Color　　　The color of the spotlight
- Tightness　The power function used to determine the shape of the hot spot
- Angle　　　The angle (in degrees) of the full effect of the spotlight
- Falloff　　A larger angle at which the amount of light falls to nothing

The following listing (Listing 5-17) shines a spotlight onto a ball and a checkered plane. The rendered image is shown in Figure 5-34. The soft edges of the light are created by the last two terms in the spotlight declaration. The angles in the spotlight declaration are specified in terms of the direction the spotlight is pointed. The interior of the spotlight, from the exact direction it is pointed to an angle of 10 degrees off from that direction, is completely white. From 10 degrees to 25 degrees the spotlight gradually fades to black.

LISTING 5-17 A BALL LIT BY A SPOTLIGHT

```
spot_light white, <10,10,0>, <3,0,0>, 3, 10, 25

// A sphere sitting on a checkered polygon
object{ sphere <0, 0, 0>, 2 shiny_red }
object {
   polygon 4, <-20,-2, -20>, <-20,-2, 20>, <20,-2, 20>, <20,-2, -20>
   texture {
     checker matte_white, matte_black
     translate <0, 0.1, 0>
     }
   }
```

Figure 5-34 Ball Lit by Spotlight

DIRECTIONAL LIGHTS

A directional light is just that. Light that comes from a particular direction. This is a way to get the effect of a very distant light source. The format of the declaration is one of these:

```
directional_light color, direction
directional_light direction
```

An important distinction of directional lights is that they do not cast shadows.

TEXTURED LIGHTS

Textured lights are an extension of positional lights that use a function to define the intensity and color of the light in each direction. The format of the declaration is

```
textured_light {
    color expression
    [scale/translate/rotate/shear]
    }
```

For an example of its use, see the disco light animation in Chapter 6, *The Movie Pages.*

BACKGROUND COLOR

The background color is the one used if the current ray does not strike any objects. The color can be any vector expression, although it is usually a simple RGB color value.

The format of the declaration is

```
background <R,G,B>
background color
```

If no background color is set, black will be used.

An interesting trick that can be performed with the background is to use an image map as the background color. Here is how this can be done:

```
background planar_imagemap(image("test1.tga", P)
```

Textures

Polyray supports a few simple procedural textures: a standard shading model, a checker texture, a hexagon texture, and a noise texture. In addition, a very flexible (although slower) functional texture is supported. The general syntax of a texture is

```
texture { [texture declaration] }
```

when a texture declaration includes a surface declaration followed by optional statements to translate, rotate or scale the texture.

SURFACES

Unlike many other raytracers, surfaces in Polyray allow you to define the color that is used for each component of the shading model. If no components are defined, Polyray defaults to a matte white.

For example, Listing 5-18 creates a red surface with a white highlight, corresponding to the often seen plastic texture.

LISTING 5-18 A RED SURFACE WITH A WHITE HIGHLIGHT

```
define shiny_red
texture {
   surface {
      ambient red, 0.2
      diffuse red, 0.6
      specular white, 0.8
      microfacet Reitz 10
      }
   }
```

The surface characteristics that can be defined are listed in Table 5-8.

Table 5-8 ∗ Polyray Surface Statements

Statement	Definition
color <r, g, b>	Basic surface color (used for any component that does not define its own color).
ambient scale ambient color, scale	Amount of ambient contribution.
diffuse scale diffuse color, scale	Diffuse contribution.

Continued on next page

119

Continued from previous page

specular scale	Amount and color of specular highlights.
specular color, scale	If the color is not given, then the body color will be used.
reflection scale	Reflectivity of the surface.
transmission scale, ior	Amount of refracted light.
transmission color, scale, ior	
microfacet kind angle	Specular lighting model. Kind: Blinn, Cook, Phong, or Reitz. Angle is the 50% falloff angle for the highlight.

See the file `colors.inc` for a number of declarations of surface characteristics, including: mirror, glass, shiny, and matte. See the Polyray documentation for more extensive descriptions of how each of the declarations are used.

CHECKER TEXTURES

The checker texture does just what its name implies— it uses two textures in a checkerboard on the associated surface. The declaration has the form

```
texture {
   checker texture1, texture2
   }
```

where `texture1` and `texture2` are texture declarations (or texture constants). A standard sort of checkered plane can be defined as shown in Listing 5-19.

LISTING 5-19 A CHECKERED PLANE

```
// Define a matte red surface
define matte_red
texture {
   surface {
      ambient red, 0.1
      diffuse red, 0.5
      }
   }

// Define a matte blue surface
define matte_blue
texture {
```

120

```
surface {
   ambient blue, 0.2
   diffuse blue, 0.8
   }
}

// Define a plane that has red and blue checkers
object {
   disc <0, 0.01, 0>, <0, 1, 0>, 5000
   texture {
      checker matte_red, matte_blue
      }
}
```

For example, see Figure 5-34, which has a plane with a black and white checker.

HEXAGON TEXTURES

The hexagon texture is oriented in the x-z plane, and has the form

```
texture {
   hexagon texture1, texture2, texture3
   }
```

This texture produces a honeycomb tiling of the three textures in the declaration. Remember that this tiling is with respect to the x-z plane; if you want it on a vertical wall, you will need to rotate the texture.

NOISE SURFACES

The noise surface is more complex and takes longer to render than the standard shading model, but is simpler and faster than the special surface described in the following section. It is an attempt to capture a large number of the standard 3-D texturing operations in a single declaration.

A noise surface declaration has the form

```
texture {
   noise surface {
      [ noise surface definition ]
      }
}
```

The allowed surface characteristics that can be defined are listed in Table 5-9.

Figure 5-35 Jade and Light
Wood Noise Surfaces

As an example of using noise surfaces to build textures, Listing 5-20 creates a jade and a light wood texture. The rendered image of this file is shown in Figure 5-35. The key distinctions between these two textures are the components `position_fn` and `color_map`. The use of a lookup that is based on location along the x-axis creates the marble-like swirls in the jade texture. The use of a cylindrical lookup function creates the rings in the light wood texture.

Table 5-9 ⋅ Polyray Noise Surface Statements

Statement	Definition
color <r, g, b>	Basic surface color (used if the noise function generates a value not contained in the color map).
ambient scale	Amount of ambient contribution.
diffuse scale	Diffuse contribution.
specular color, scale	Amount and color of specular highlights. If the color is not given then the body color will be used.
reflection scale	Reflectivity of the surface.
transmission scale, ior	Amount of refracted light.
microfacet kind angle	Specular lighting model.
color_map (map_entries)	Define the color map.
bump_scale fexper	How much the bumpiness affects the normal.
frequency fexper	Affects the wavelength of ripples and waves.
phase fexper	Affects the phase of the ripples and waves.

lookup_fn index	Selects a predefined lookup function.
normal_fn index	Selects a predefined normal modifier.
octaves fexper	Number of octaves of noise to use.
position_fn index	How the intersection point is used in the process of generating a noise texture.
position_scale fexper	Amount of contribution of the position value to the overall texture.
turbulence fexper	Amount of contribution of the noise to overall texture.

The entries in the color map affect only the color of the texture, not the patterns within the texture. By adjusting the color values in the maps, it would be possible to make the rings in the wood darker, or to change from a green jade to an orange marble. See Listing 5-20, which shows the code for JADE.PI.

LISTING 5-20 JADE.PI

```
viewpoint {
    from <0,15,-25>
    at <0,4,0>
    up <0,1,0>
    angle 30
    resolution 80, 60
    aspect 4/3
    }

background white
light 0.8*white, <-10, 10, -20>
light 0.8*white, < 10, 10, -20>

define position_objectx      1
define position_cylindrical 3
define lookup_sawtooth 1

define jade
texture {
  noise surface {
      ambient 0.3
      diffuse 0.8
      specular 0.4
      microfacet Reitz 5
      position_fn position_objectx
      lookup_fn    lookup_sawtooth
```

continued on next page

continued from previous page

```
        octaves     3
        turbulence  3
        color_map(
           [0.0, 0.8, <0.1, 0.6, 0.1>, <0.0, 0.3, 0.0>]
           [0.8, 1.0, <0.1, 0.6, 0.1>, <0.0, 0.2, 0.0>])
        }
     rotate <80, 0, 0>
     scale <3, 3, 3>
     }

define light_wood
texture {
   noise surface {
      ambient 0.2
      diffuse 0.7
      specular white, 0.5
      microfacet Reitz 10
      position_fn position_cylindrical
      position_scale 1
      lookup_fn lookup_sawtooth
      octaves 3
      turbulence 1
      color_map(
         [0.0, 0.8, <1, 0.72, 0.25>, <1, 0.72, 0.25>]
         [0.8, 1.0, <0.5, 0.5, 0.07>, <0.4, 0.4, 0.035>])
         }
   // scale <2, 2, 2>
   }

define vase
object {
   lathe 2, <0, 1, 0>, 12,
      <0, 0>, <2, 0>,   <3.5, 1>,   <3.5, 2>,   <1, 7>,   <3.5, 8>,
      <2, 8>, <0.5, 7>, <2.5, 2>, <2.5, 1>, <2, 0.5>, <0, 0.5>
   }

// Make a jade vase
vase { jade translate <-4.5, 0, 0> }
vase { light_wood translate <4.5, 0, 0> }
```

A wide variety of effects are possible with noise surfaces. For more detailed descriptions of how these textures work and how to go about creating and modifying them, see the files TEXTURE.TXT and POLYRAY.DOC in the Polyray document archives.

SPECIAL SURFACES

The most general texture is the special surface. These textures are evaluated at run-time based on the expressions given for the components of the lighting model. The general syntax for a surface using a functional texture is

```
special surface {
   [ surface declaration ]
   }
```

The surface declarations are the same as those of the standard shading model. In addition to the components usually defined in a surface declaration, it is possible to define a function that deflects the normal, and a body color that will be used as the color filter in the ambient, diffuse, etc., components of the surface declaration. The formats of the two declarations are

```
color  vexper
normal vexper
```

Listing 5-21 is an example of how a functional texture can be defined. The rendered image of a sphere using this texture is shown in Figure 5-36.

LISTING 5-21 DEFINING A FUNCTIONAL TEXTURE
```
define sin_color_offset (sin(3.14 * fmod(2*x*y*z, 1)) + 1) / 2

    define xyz_sin_texture
    texture {
      special surface {
        color sin_color_offset * white
        ambient 0.2
        diffuse 0.7
        specular white, 0.4
        microfacet Cook 10
        }
      }
```

Figure 5-36 Sin Wave Special Surface

125

In this example, the color of the surface is defined based on the location of the intersection point using the vector defined as `sin_color_offset`.

One use for a functional texture is to create an image map. Polyray supports several forms of image maps: planar, cylindrical, spherical, and environmental. To associate an image with a surface, the image is used as the `color` component of the functional texture. At run-time, the image is accessed to determine what the color of the surface should be. See the Polyray documents, as well as the sample data files for descriptions and examples of image mapping.

As the last example in this chapter, Listing 5-22 demonstrates how to build an environment map and how to use it in a texture declaration. The purpose of an environment map is to give the illusion of reflectivity to a surface by building images of all the things that surround the surface, then wrapping those images around the surface.

LISTING 5-22 BUILDING AN ENVIRONMENT MAP

```
// location will be set to the position that the environment map
// is being built for.  The origin is used here only as an example.
define location <0, 0, 0>

// The next two arrays define the orientation of each of 6 views
// from location.
define at_vecs [<1, 0, 0>, <-1, 0, 0>, < 0, 1, 0>, < 0,-1, 0>,
                < 0, 0, 1>, < 0, 0,-1>]
define up_vecs [< 0, 1, 0>, < 0, 1, 0>, < 0, 0, 1>, < 0, 0,-1>,
                < 0, 1, 0>, < 0, 1, 0>]

// Generate six frames, one in each direction
start_frame 0
end_frame 5
outfile view

// Each frame generates the view in a specific direction.  The
// vectors stored in the arrays at_vecs, and "up_vecs" turn the
// camera in such a way as to generate image maps correct for using
// in an environment map.
viewpoint {
   from location
   at location + at_vecs[frame]
   up up_vecs[frame]
   angle 90
   ...
   }
```

```
...
The rest of the file would contain the objects that will be rendered into the
environment maps.
...
```

Figure 5-37 shows the arrangement of an environment map. The numbers on the faces of the cube represent the view orientations generated by the corresponding entries in the arrays at_vecs and up_vecs previously listed.

An environment map typically is used to give the appearance of reflectivity to an object. Assuming that the environment map was generated from the center of the sphere below (the vector <1,17,30> was used for the definition of location above), the following statements would wrap the environment map around it:

```
object {
    sphere <1, 17, 30>, 1
    texture {
        special surface {
            color environment_map(environment("view000.tga", "view001.tga",
                                               "view002.tga", "view003.tga",
                                               "view004.tga", "view005.tga"))
            ambient 0.2
            diffuse 0.8
        }
    }
}
```

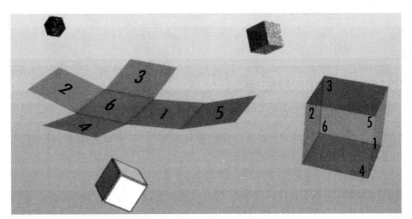

Figure 5-37 Environment Map

DTA

Once you have rendered a series of picture files, you will need to be able to display them very quickly. You could use a display program to load and display each picture sequentially, but that would be far too slow to create an effective illusion of movement. It takes too much time to read a picture from disk and update the whole screen.

DTA (Dave's TGA Animator) assembles all of your pictures in a single flic file, which stores only the differences between the frames in an animation. If you've got enough memory in your PC, a player program can load an entire flic into memory, completely eliminating the disk overhead. It also takes a lot less time to update only a portion of the screen.

SHAREWARE INFORMATION

DTA is a shareware program that may be freely distributed in unmodified form for evaluation purposes. If you use it frequently, you are requested to pay a registration fee of $35. To register, send the fee to the author:

David K. Mason
P.O. Box 181015
Boston, MA 02118

INSTALLATION

Installation instructions for DTA are contained in Chapter 1, *Introduction*. The rest of this section assumes that the files have been installed according to those instructions.

SYSTEM REQUIREMENTS

Two executable files are included with this book:

- DTA.EXE, which operates in real mode. It requires at least an 80286-based computer. This version can access only conventional memory. This is usually sufficient for generating flics at 320x200 pixels.

- DTAX.EXE, which operates in 286 protected mode. It requires at least an 80286-based system. It requires at least 2MB of memory and can access up to 16 MB. For it to be accessible by DTAX, the memory must either be configured as XMS memory (Extended Memory Specification, set up with HIMEM.SYS or a similar program) or raw (no memory-management drivers). DTAX will not be able to see any memory that you configure as EMS (Expanded Memory Specification, set up with EMM386.SYS or a similar product).

CREATING A SIMPLE FLIC

Let's assume you have created a bunch of Targa files using Polyray, and you want to turn them into a flic. The easiest way is to type the DTA command with a wildcard file name, like this:

```
dta *.tga
```

This command causes DTA to go through all the .TGA files in the current directory. DTA scans your pictures to figure out which colors they contain, generates a 256-color VGA palette, and then crunches the pictures into a flic file. This works correctly only if the names of your files are in a sequence, like FILE000.TGA, FILE001.TGA, FILE003.TGA, and so forth, because DTA sorts the file names before processing. Also, there can be no .TGA pictures in the current directory other than the ones you want to go in the animation.

What if you have other pictures in the current directory and would rather not move them elsewhere? You can use a more specific, wildcard file specification, like this one:

```
dta file*.tga
```

DTA still processes all of the files in your sequence, but it ignores all picture files that do not begin with FILE.

If you don't want to use a wildcard as in the last two examples, you can specify each of your files by name. They'll be added to your new flic in the order you typed them:

```
dta first.tga second.tga last.tga
```

That gets boring fast if you have a lot of images, so DTA provides one more method of specifying files. You can create, with your text editor, a text file containing the names of the pictures that you want to compile into a flic. Let's say you create a file called PICS.LST, that looks like this:

```
pic003.tga
pic004.tga
pic002.tga
pic001.tga
```

You can tell DTA to process the pictures listed by supplying it with the name of the list file, preceded by an "@":

```
dta @pics.lst
```

DTA will create a flic using the files listed, in the order that they occur in the file. You can include any of the file types listed under the section below. You can't include another list file.

FILES DTA CAN READ

DTA can read many kinds of files and convert them into a single flic. The most popular true-color format in the PC raytracing world is called the Targa (TGA for short) format, and was originally designed by Truevision for use with their Targa graphics boards. TGA files come in 8-, 16-, 24-, and 32-bit versions, compressed and uncompressed. Because this is the only type of image file that Polyray and DMorf create, you'll be seeing a lot of them. DTA can also read

- .GIF files — The CompuServe Graphics Interchange format is the most common format for 256-color pictures. DTA can read both the GIF87a and GIF89a varieties.

- .IMG files — Created by Stephen Coy's Vivid raytracer.

- .PCX files — Originally designed for ZSOFT's PC Paintbrush program, PCX has developed into a standard graphics file format, supported by many applications. It comes in several varieties, supporting everything from black and white pictures up to 24-bit pictures. DTA can read only the 256-color and 24-bit varieties.

DTA can also process standard compressed archive files. These are just containers for picture files. Archive formats that DTA supports are

➥ .LZH — Created with Haruyasu Yoshizaki's LHA archiving program. A copy of LHA.EXE must be on your disk, in a directory that's in your DOS path, for DTA to read pictures from these files.

➥ .ZIP — Created with PKWare's PKZIP archiving program. You will have to have a copy of PKUNZIP.EXE for DTA to be able to read these.

➥ .ARJ — Created with Robert Jung's ARJ archiving program. You must have a copy of ARJ.EXE for DTA to be able to read these files.

COMMAND LINE SWITCHES

Sometimes the settings that DTA selects by default won't give you the results you want. You can make DTA operate differently by entering switches on the DTA command line. Every switch begins with a (/) or a dash (-) so that DTA will know it isn't a file name. The switches for DTA *are not* case-sensitive.

Output File (/F)

By default, DTA will create a flic file from your input pictures. You can change that with the /F switch. Table 5-10 illustrates which formats DTA can create, and the switches you'll need to specify.

Table 5-10 ➥ Supported Output Formats

Switch	Output Format
/FG	GIF (CompuServe Graphics Interchange Format)
/FT	TGA (Targa) format
/FM	MAP palette format (used by Fractint and Piclab)
/FC	COL palette format (used by Autodesk Animator)

Set File Name (/O)

If you don't tell it otherwise, DTA will create a flic called ANIM.FLI. You could tell it to change the name to SOMETHNG.FLI by using the /O switch, like this:

```
C> dta *.tga /osomethng
```

Resolution (/R#)

If you don't provide a resolution switch, then DTA will create a flic that's 320 pixels across by 200 pixels. That's the resolution of the original .FLI file format from Autodesk Animator. It's also the only resolution supported by a number of flic players, such as AAPLAY, AADEMO, and QUICKFLI.

DTA will allow you to create a flic with a different resolution by typing a /R switch. Table 5-11 lists available resolutions and the switches you can use to select them.

Table 5-11 ⁎ Resolution Switches

Switch	Resolution
/R1	320 * 200 (default)
/R2	320 * 240
/R3	320 * 400
/R4	320 * 480
/R5	360 * 480
/R6	640 * 480
/R7	640 * 400
/R8	800 * 600
/R10	1024 * 768
/R12	1280 * 1024

In addition, you can use /RA to create a flic file of the same resolution as your TGA files, whatever that might be.

If you use any resolution other than 320x200, DTA will create an .FLC file instead of an .FLI file.

Speed (/S#)

By default, DTA will put a "speed" value of 0 into your flic file. This tells the flic-player to move the frames of your animation to the screen as fast as it possibly can.

If that's too fast, you can change the speed value using the /S value.

If you're creating a 320x200 .FLI (the original Autodesk Animator format), then the number you type following the /S represents a number of 1/70ths of a second. So if you type /S5, the screen will be updated no more than fourteen times per second. If you're creating an .FLC, then the speed value represents a number of milliseconds.

In some cases, the information content (the change per frame) exceeds what your hardware can support. In that case, the speed is governed by factors such as the speed of data transfer to VGA memory and, when there isn't enough RAM to hold the entire flic, disk access. If disk access is the bottleneck, you can sometimes speed things up by defragmenting your hard disk with a product like the SPEEDISK program that comes with Symantec's Norton Utilities.

Color Selection

In a true-color image (like the pictures you create in Polyray and DMorf), each pixel's color is made up of three numbers, which represent red, green, and blue. Each of these values can be any number from 0 to 255. So there are 16,777,216 distinct possible colors. One 320x200 picture might contain as many as 64,000 different colors. A 640x480 picture could contain 307,200 different colors.

Unfortunately, VGA monitors can display only 256 colors on the screen at a time, so DTA must pick 256 colors that approximate all of the colors in all of the images. To do this, DTA uses a gimmick called *Octree Quantization*, a quick and low-memory-overhead alternative to such common color-reduction methods as Popularity and Median-Cut. DTA scans each of your pictures to find out what colors they contain, and then it selects the best 256 to use in the flic. This method produces the best palette that DTA is capable of creating.

GRAYSCALE PALETTES (/G AND /G32)

If you use the /G switch, DTA will create a palette of 64 shades of gray instead of using color. If you use the /G32 switch, DTA will use a palette of 32 shades of gray. This is probably only useful if you're going to display your animations on a laptop with a grayscale display. Many laptops can display only 32 shades. DTA can create grayscale flics much more quickly than it can if it uses color, because there's no need to scan all of the pictures first or search through a tree to pick colors.

3/3/2 PALETTE (/332)

If you select the /332 switch, DTA will use a palette containing combinations of eight shades of red, eight shades of green, and four shades of blue. (It's called a 3/3/2 palette because that's how many bits are used for each color component.) Animations that use this palette look rather dreadful, but DTA can create them very quickly.

EXTERNAL PALETTE (/U)

If you have a palette file created outside of DTA (or created with DTA), in the .COL (Autodesk Animator) or .MAP (PICLAB/Fractint) format, then you can tell DTA to use that palette with the /U switch, like this:

```
C> dta *.tga /uneon.map
```

Instead of generating its own palette based on the colors in the image, DTA will use the set of colors defined in the palette file NEON.MAP.

ORIGINAL PALETTE (/NM)

If you're starting with a collection of 256-color .GIF or .PCX files, which already have a palette, instead of .TGAs, then you can tell DTA not to create a new palette at all with the /NM switch. DTA will use the palette of the first picture in the group, and won't remap any of the colors. Don't use this trick if your 256-color images contain different palettes, unless you really enjoy digital noise.

Dithering

Frequently, an image won't look as good as the original after DTA has reduced the number of colors in it. When some small detail of your picture has an unpopular color (meaning, that color doesn't appear very much in the picture), it will often end up mapped to the wrong color. For example, imagine you create a picture containing one yellow banana in a bowl of oranges on a brown table in the middle of a tan room. All of these colors are fairly close to each other in the spectrum, and when DTA decides which shades in the yellow/orange/tan area to use, it is going to pick the more popular shades. Chances are, you are going to end up with an orange, brown, or tan banana.

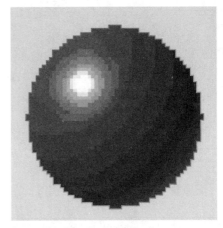

Figure 5-38 Color Banding

Groups of different but similar colors are reduced to a single color, so any areas in your pictures containing a smooth gradation from one color to another will end up as several bands of discrete shades, as you can see illustrated in Figure 5-38.

We can use a technique called *dithering* to trick your eye into seeing more colors than are actually there. Although each individual pixel might contain an incorrect color, a group of pixels will approximate the right colors. DTA provides several methods of dithering your picture: Floyd-Steinberg, Sierra-Lite, Ordered, and Random noise.

FLOYD-STEINBERG AND SIERRA-LITE (/DF AND /DS)

Floyd-Steinberg (/DF) and Sierra-Lite (/DS) are both *error-diffusion* dithering methods. They both work as follows.

Whenever DTA can't make a perfect match between an input color and an output color, it

1. Calculates the difference, in red/green/blue values, between the two colors (the *error*).

2. Divides the error into smaller chunks.

3. Subtracts the error chunks from the colors of some of the other pixels in the neighborhood.

DTA then uses the modified colors to select the output colors for those pixels.

Figure 5-39 Sample Error-Diffusion Dither

The only difference between F-S and S-L dithering is how many pixels receive part of the error. F-S modifies four pixels, and S-L modifies two.

Of all the dithering methods that DTA supplies, these error-diffusion techniques tend to produce the nicest looking output (see Figure 5-39). On the other hand, error diffusion doesn't work very well with flic compression. Even if there are only minor differences between the TGA files for two frames in an animation, error-diffusion dithering can result in large differences in the flic frames...and very large and slowly playing flics. So only use /DF and /DS if you've got plenty of disk space and a fast computer.

Figure 5-40 Sample Ordered Dither

ORDERED DITHERING (/DO#)

Ordered dithering works by imposing a "pattern" on a picture. It adds or subtracts numbers from a pattern table to the colors in the input picture. It can be described as viewing your flic through a screen door.

The number that you can enter along with the /DO switch represents the "strength" of the pattern, or how big the numbers that are used to modify the colors can be. /DO1 adds a very light pattern to your pictures. /DO7 can make your animation look a lot like a bad tapestry, as shown in Figure 5-40. If you don't enter any number with /DO, then DTA will behave as if you had specified a value of seven.

Ordered dithering won't cause the size of your flic to expand nearly as much as error-diffusion dithering. That's because the numbers it uses to filter your images will always be the same from one frame to another. But it will still be larger than a nondithered flic.

RANDOM NOISE DITHERING (/DR#)

Random noise dithering works a lot like ordered dithering, except instead of using a pattern, it just modifies the colors in your picture with numbers that it makes up as it goes along. The number you enter along with the /DR switch represents the maximum size of the random numbers. The default, eight, works well most of the time.

Instead of making your pictures look like needlepoint, the random dither adds a grainy look. Take a look at Figure 5-41 for an example.

Figure 5-41 Sample Random Noise Dither

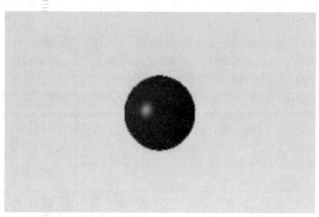

Figure 5-42 No Scaling

The "random" numbers that DTA filters your pictures with aren't really random. They'll stay the same from one frame to the next, so your flics won't grow nearly as huge as they would with error-diffusion dithering. Dithered regions remain fixed from frame to frame.

Picture Scaling (/SC)

When you build a flic from pictures that are smaller than the screen size, DTA will center them on the screen, and fill the rest of the screen with a black border. Figure 5-42 shows a 100x100 picture displayed on a 320x200 screen.

Sometimes this will look just fine, but other times you'll want to use more of the screen's real estate. You can use the /SC switch to resize the pictures to fill the whole screen:

```
C:\> dta sph*.tga /sc
```

DTA will scale the pictures to the screen's dimensions (320x200 if you don't use the /R switch). Take a look at Figure 5-43 for the result.

Sometimes you'll want to resize the picture, but not to the exact dimensions of the screen. In the current example, scaling a 100x100 picture to 320x200 warps the picture of a sphere so it looks like a deflated beach ball. So DTA allows you to supply it with a specific size:

```
dta sph*.tga /sc200,200
```

and DTA will scale to the 200x200 instead of 320x200. See Figure 5-44.

Figure 5-43 Scaling with /SC

Frame Averaging (/A# and /T#)

In computer animation generated with Polyray, a single frame represents only a single instant in time. In live-action film, a frame represents a short but measureable length of time. You can see the effect of this difference when you press the pause button on a VCR while an object is moving very quickly across the TV screen. You'll see a blur across the area where the object moves between one frame and the next. This effect is called *motion blur*. In each frame from a computer animation, the object will appear perfectly clear (see Figure 5-43), regardless of how much it moves.

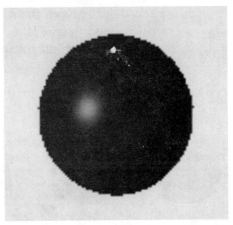

Figure 5-44 Scaling with /SC200,200

Figure 5-45 No Motion Blur

DTA allows you to get a fake motion blur effect by averaging multiple frames. Just use the /A switch, along with a number representing a number of frames to average:

```
C:\>dta *.tga /a3
```

and DTA will create a flic in which every group of three input pictures will be combined into a single frame. Of course, this means you'll have to create three times as many pictures. By default (if you use /A without a number), DTA will average two frames. See Figure 5-46 for an example of a sequence of 25 pictures crunched down to a 5-frame flic with /A5.

The /T (trail) option works much like the /A switch, but creates a new frame from every input picture. The sequence created with /T3 looks like 1-2 3, 2-3-4, 3-4-5, instead of 1-2-3, 4-5-6, 7-8-9.

Skipping Frames (/C, /K)

If you have a large number of frames in an animation project, it can take DTA a long time to process them. DTA must first scan every single picture to build a palette, and then read them all over again when it builds a flic. You can speed things up by instructing DTA to ignore some of the frames while it's building a palette with the /C switch:

```
C:\> dta *.tga /c5
```

Figure 5-46 Motion Blur

DTA will then scan only once for every five pictures. Because sequential frames almost always share very similar colors, the palette will usually look just as good. Don't use this feature if your colors vary widely from frame to frame. If you use the /C switch without supplying a number, DTA will assume you meant /C2.

The /K switch tells DTA not to use some of the frames at all, making your flic shorter. If you type the following command:

```
C:\> DTA *.tga /k3
```

DTA will use only one of every three pictures. If you start with 30 TGA files, the resulting flic will contain only ten frames. If you don't supply a number along with the /K switch, DTA will assume that you meant /K2, and will skip every other picture. If you use both the /C and /K parameters:

```
C:\> DTA *.tga /k2 /c3
```

DTA will skip every other picture, and of the remaining pictures it will scan only one picture out of three to build the palette. If you start with 12 pictures, then only pictures 0 and 6 will be used for palette pictures, and only pictures 0, 2, 4, 6, 8, and 10 will show up in the flic.

Frame Expansion (/X#)

If the motion in your flic looks too jumpy or jerky, that's probably because you didn't render enough frames. The best way to correct the problem would be to go back to the drawing board and re-render twice as many frames. If you're in a rush, you can use the /X switch instead:

```
C:\> dta *.tga /x
```

DTA will create a flic containing an extra averaged frame between each pair of regular frames in your flic. If you want more than a single extra frame, add a number after the "/X."

Ping-Pong (/P)

Earlier in the book we talked about *looping*, which means making sure that the end of a flic is the same as the beginning. This prevents the animation from skipping when a flic player finishes playing it and starts it up again. If you have a non-looping set of pictures, DTA can fix that by using the ping-pong effect. DTA adds each of your pictures to the animation, then it adds each of the frames again to the end in reverse order. If you start out with five frames in the animation, for example, the ping-pong flic will insert the pictures in the order 1-2-3-4-5-4-3-2.

3-D (/3D)

The /3D option tells DTA to create a red/blue 3-D effect, the kind that you need those special red-and-blue 3-D glasses to see. Assuming you have got a collection of Targa files labeled LEFT000.TGA, LEFT001.TGA, and so on, which should be used for the image that the left eye sees, and another collection labeled RGHT000.TGA, RGHT001.TGA, etc., which should be used for the image that the right eye sees, then run DTA with this command line:

```
C:\> dta left*.tga rght*.tga /3d /o3d
```

DTA will generate a flic called 3D.FLI. All the images from the "LEFT" series of Targas are displayed in red, and all the "RGHT" pictures are displayed in blue.

Note that you can't use just any combination of pictures to produce a nice 3-D effect. You'll have to generate two sets of pictures in Polyray, with the camera positions spaced apart from each other. In addition, the points that the cameras are looking at must be separated by the same amount of space as the "eyes." It will take some experimentation to get it just right.

Creating Targa Files (/NC, /B)

By default, when DTA creates a Targa file (with /FT) it will compress it using run-length encoding. Unfortunately, not all applications that can read Targas know how to read the compressed ones. In which case, tell DTA not to compress by using the /NC (no compression) option. DTA's other Targa-related default is to create them using 24-bit color. You can tell it to create 16-bit Targas with /B16, or 32-bit Targas with /B32.

TRILOBYTE PLAY

Although you've built all of your TGA files with Polyray or DMorf, and translated them into a flic with DTA, you still haven't seen anything move. For that, you need the Play program from Trilobyte. Play can load even large flics completely into memory and display them *fast*.

SHAREWARE INFORMATION

Play is not a free program. If you find it useful and continue using it after you've tried it out, you must make a registration payment of $39.00 to

Trilobyte
P.O. Box 1412
Jacksonville, OR 97530

Registered users will receive the latest version of Play and also Groovie, a program that builds scripts for Play.

RUNNING PLAY

To run Play, just use the command "PLAY" and the name of the flic file that you want to display:

```
C:\> play some.fli
```

or

```
C:\> play some.flc
```

Play will display that flic on your screen at the speed value that's stored inside the flic's header. When you have finished watching, press the (ESC) key to exit.

Changing Speed

If the flic is moving too slow or too fast, you can alter the playback speed by pressing the number keys on your keyboard, from (1) to (9). The number 1 causes Play to display the flic as fast as it's able. If you press (9), Play will display it very slowly.

You can also affect the playback speed by using the -S (or /S) command line switch with a number from 0 to 255, like this:

```
C:\> play some.fli -s20
```

A number specified with -S works the same as a speed value built into a flic. In a 320x200 .FLI file, it represents a number of *jiffies*, or 1/70s of a second, to spend on each frame. In a .FLC file, it represents a number of milliseconds per frame.

Looping

By default, Play will keep on displaying your flic forever, or at least until you press the (ESC) key. You can make Play run it a specified number of times, with the "-l" (loop) command line switch:

```
C:\> play some.fli -l5
```

This causes Play to display the flic five times, and then exit to a DOS command line.

Changing Luminosity

If you display a movie, and the colors are too dark or too light, you can adjust the brightness by pressing the (PG UP) and (PG DN) keys. (PG UP) will brighten things up, and (PG DN) will make the flic darker.

HARDWARE REQUIREMENTS

Play can display low-resolution (320x200) flics on any VGA display, or higher-resolution (640x480) flics on pretty much any Super-VGA display. For resolutions higher than 640x480, you must have either a VESA (Video Electronics Standards Association) compliant SVGA board, or VESA driver software.

Play likes to load entire flics into memory before displaying them. If it can't load the whole thing into memory, then playback will be much slower. If your flics are too large for conventional memory, make sure you have plenty of expanded memory (EMS) available, using a driver like EMM386.SYS or QEMM386.SYS. Play does not support extended memory (XMS). Recent versions of some memory managers, including QEMM-386, can allocate your memory as both EMS and XMS simultaneously. This is ideal, since the other programs included with this book support XMS instead of EMS.

SP

If you recall the discussion of complex paths in Chapter 4, *Advanced Techniques,* you've seen Polyray move objects in some very unusual ways. Spline paths are probably the most interesting of the path types, but they're also the most difficult to set up. You've got to figure out such items as multiple start and end points and relative velocities. SP (Dave's Spline-Path Generator) is a utility that handles most of that for you. If you supply it with a list of points, SP will come up with a curvy 3-D path that passes through each of those points, and return a set of rotations and translations that will move an object along that path.

Because SP is external to Polyray, you can't use Polyray's automatic frame counter the same way you would if everything was in your data file. For every frame of your animation, you need to execute SP and then execute Polyray. It would be a drag to have to type in all those commands manually, so SP comes with a DOS batch (.BAT) file that will do the typing for you.

BUILDING A PATH

To define a spline path, you must create a text file containing a list of 3-D coordinates. These coordinates, or *control points,* define a curve that passes through each point. Here's a simple example of an SP path file, called CURVE.PTH:

```
<-2,0,0>
<1,2,0>
<-1,2,0>
<2,0,0>
```

These control points define the curve in Figure 5-47. Because the z-coordinates for all of the control points are set to zero, the curve will lie flat in the z-plane.

RUNNING SP

If you run the SP program with this command line:

```
C:\> sp curve.pth /t10 /f2
```

you are telling the SP program to generate all the values needed to place an object in position for the second frame of a 10-frame animation using our path. It places these definitions in an include file with the same file name as

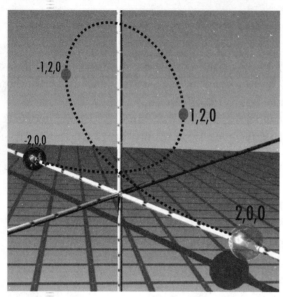

Figure 5-47 The Spline Path Defined by CURVE.PTH

the path file, but with an extension of .INC. In this case, we'd get a file called CURVE.INC that looks like this:

```
define CURVE_LOC <0.97557,1.51971,0.0>
define CURVE_YR1 <-0.50565>
define CURVE_ZR  <26.30300>
define CURVE_YR2 <180.0000>
```

Because SP uses the name of the path file as a prefix for each of these variables, you could have multiple paths coexisting in the same animation. These values are all you need to place an object in position 20 percent of the way along the spline curve. To use these values in a Polyray data file, you would insert an `include` statement at the top of your data file:

```
include "CURVE.INC"
```

Define the object that you want to move along the curve. The object must be centered on the world origin, and it must point upward (in the positive direction along the z-axis) for this to work right. If you use a symmetrical object like a box or sphere, the orientation doesn't matter, so just use a box:

```
object {
  box <-0.25,-0.25,-0.25>,<0.25,0.25,0.25>
  shiny_red
}
```

Next, using the variables defined by SP, insert a series of transformation statements into the object definition:

```
object {
  box <-0.25,-0.25,-0.25>,<0.25,0.25,0.25>
  shiny_red
  rotate <0,CURVE_YR1,CURVE_ZR>
  rotate <0,CURVE_YR2,0>
  translate CURVE_LOC
}
```

The two `rotate` statements pivot the object so that it's pointing along the axis of the curve. The `translate` moves the object into its final position. If you don't want your object to turn as it moves along the curve, just omit the `rotate`. Figure 5-48 illustrates how the statements transform the object.

THE BATCH FILE

If we run Polyray now, we'll end up with an object that remains at two-tenths of the way along the curve axis. Polyray knows how to update its own frame counters, but it can't make SP generate values for new positions. So we'll use a DOS batch program to run SP and Polyray once for every frame in the animation.

Figure 5-48 Rotating and Translating the Box

Even if you're new to the DOS/PC world, you've seen at least one batch program, a file called AUTOEXEC.BAT. It executes a list of commands every time you turn on your PC or reboot it. But batch files are capable of doing quite a bit more than just executing a string of commands in sequence. You can use variables, conditional execution of commands, loops, and more. You can't do math very easily in a batch file, but a batch file can always call another program to do the math for it. For that purpose, the batch file comes with a program called ADD1.EXE. All ADD1 does is to increment a numeric variable by one.

CURVE.BAT (shown in Listing 5-23) is a sample batch file that is designed to run SP (or, with modifications, any similar program) along with Polyray a specified number of times.

LISTING 5-23 CURVE.BAT

```
@echo off

rem Accept one command-line parameter, specifying which frame number
rem to begin the loop with.  If no parameter is supplied, start with
rem frame 0.

 if '%1'=='' goto initfr
 SET FRAME=%1
 goto setlim
:initfr
 SET FRAME=0

rem Accept a second command-line parameter, specifying a total number
rem of frames to generate.

 if '%2'=='' goto setlim
 SET LIMIT=%2
 goto loop
:setlim
 SET LIMIT=30

rem Execute the following lines for every frame in the animation

:loop

rem if all of the frames have been processed, exit the batch file

  if '%FRAME%'=='%LIMIT%' goto loopdone

rem create a file called FRMINFO.INC containing the Polyray animation settings

  echo total_frames %LIMIT% >frminfo.inc
  echo start_frame %FRAME% >>frminfo.inc
```

```
    echo end_frame %FRAME% >>frminfo.inc
    @echo on

rem Call SP

    sp curve.pth /F%FRAME% /T%LIMIT% /Q

rem Call Polyray

    polyray box.pi
    @echo off

rem increment the frame counter

    add1 FRAME
    goto loop
:loopdone
```

If you adapt this batch file for your own projects, you'll have to change a few lines. You'll need to change the names of the path file specified in the call to SP, and the data file specified in the call to Polyray.

In place of the regular animation statements that set `total_frames`, `start_frame`, and `end_frame`, insert the following line at the top of your Polyray data file:

```
include "frminfo.inc"
```

You will still be able to access the `frame` and `total_frames` variables in your data file. They are set by the FRMINFO.INC file created by CURVE.BAT. Your finished data file, BOX.PI, should look like Listing 5-24.

LISTING 5-24 BOX.PI

```
//animation settings
include "frminfo.inc"

//library files
include "colors.inc"
include "texture.inc"

//grab path variables
include "curve.inc"

//name the output files
outfile curve

//define a camera
viewpoint {
```

continued on next page

continued from previous page

```
    from <0,1,-3>
    at <0,1,0>
    up <0,1,0>
    angle 45
    hither 1
    resolution 160,100
    aspect 1.333333
    }

// And a light source
light <-10, 10, -10>

// Define an object
object {
  box <-0.25,-0.25,-0.25>,<0.25,0.25,0.25>
  shiny_red
  rotate <0,CURVE_YR1,CURVE_ZR>
  rotate <0,CURVE_YR2,0>
  translate CURVE_LOC
}
```

RUNNING CURVE.BAT

Make sure that you've got the following files: CURVE.BAT, CURVE.PTH, and BOX.PI (they are in the \MOVIES\CHAP5 directory, if you don't want to create them from scratch), SP.EXE, and ADD1.EXE (the last two can be found in the \MOVIES\TOOLS directory). Switch to \MOVIES\CHAP5 directory, and type:

```
C:\CHAP5\SP> CURVE
```

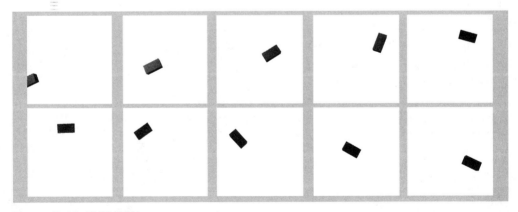

Figure 5-49 CURVE.FLI

The batch file will execute both SP and Polyray 30 times, each time generating a TGA file. Turn them into a flic with DTA, display with PLAY, and voila, you end up with Figure 5-49.

ACCELERATION

By default, SP divides its spline curves into equal pieces. Objects move at a constant speed along the curve. You can change this by adding `percent` parameters to points in a path file:

```
<-2,0,0>
<1,2,0> percent 50
<-1,2,0>
<2,0,0>
```

The `percent 50` tells SP that the object must reach the coordinate <1,2,0>, which is exactly halfway through the animation. The box will follow the same path as in the previous example, but instead of traveling at a uniform speed, it will start slowly and speed up as it goes. Figure 5-50 shows how `percent` affects the speed of the moving box.

You can add `percent` to any point in your path file except the first or last. The first coordinate always has a percent value of 0, and the last is always set to 100.

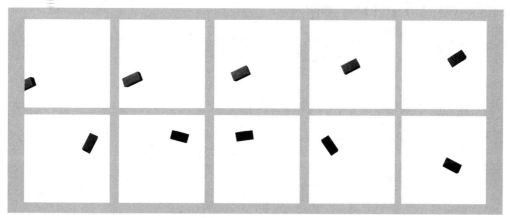

Figure 5-50 An Accelerating Box

DMORF

In recent years, you must have seen innumerable examples of the two-dimensional image morphing technique pioneered by those wizards at Industrial Light and Magic — unless you've been living in a cave. It showed up first in the motion picture *Willow,* in which a character was transformed into a series of different animals, one after another. It was also used in *Indiana Jones and the Last Crusade* (remember when the villain shrivels up after touching the Holy Grail?), and there was a ton of morphing in *Terminator 2*. Television commercials are another morphing showcase, with cars turning into tigers, cars turning into other cars, and so on. With DMorf (Dave's Morphing program), you can produce the same kind of effects.

Morphing is a simple technique for creating a series of images that transition from a beginning image to a final image. Take two still pictures, and map the features of the objects in each picture. Some morphing programs, including DMorf, use a mesh of curved lines to match the contours of the objects. Some other programs use other mechanisms. In a series of increments, warp both pictures so the matching features line up. At the same time, fade from the first picture to the second.

This section will give you a quick introduction to the DMorf program, and will suggest a few ways that you can use it to create effects that you can use in your flics. Because this book focuses on 3-D animation, the examples in this section will use computer-generated pictures of 3-D objects, but the morphing technique works just as well using scanned photographs.

SHAREWARE INFORMATION

DMorf is a shareware program that may be freely distributed in unmodified form for evaluation purposes. If you use it frequently, you are requested to pay a registration fee of $35. To register, send the fee to the author:

David K. Mason
P.O. Box 181015
Boston, MA 02118

HARDWARE REQUIREMENTS

To use DMorf at all, you *must* have

- At least a VGA display.
- At least 1MB of memory.
- A Microsoft-compatible mouse.
- At least a 286-based computer.

If you can manage it, you *should* have:

- A numeric coprocessor. Without one, DMorf is a terribly slow program. If your PC has a 486DX or DX2 chip in it, then the coprocessor is built in.

- Lots more memory. During the warping process, DMorf allocates a chunk of memory large enough to hold one entire picture in four bytes-per-pixel form. That means 256,000 bytes if you're working on 320x200 pictures, or 1,228,800 for 640x480 pictures, 1,920,000 for 800x600 pictures, or 3,145,728 for 1024x768. And that's just for storing pictures. DMorf uses memory for other purposes, too.

REQUIRED FILES

Make sure that DMORF.EXE, DPMI16BI.OVL, and RTM.EXE are all in your current directory or in a directory that's in your DOS path. If any one of these files is missing, DMorf will not work.

STARTING DMORF

The first step in morphing is deciding what to morph. You'll need to pick two pictures, in .TGA or .GIF format. The two files don't have to be in the same format, but they do have to have the same dimensions. You'll get the most convincing results if the objects in the pictures you transform have similar backgrounds, positions, and shading. For our first project, let's use pictures of some basic 3-D objects—a box and a sphere. Figure 5-51 displays the images we'll be morphing.

Figure 5-51 BOX.TGA and SPHERE.TGA

Start DMorf with this command:

```
C:\> dmorf sphere box
```

DMorf will read the pictures from disk and display them on the screen. Figure 5-52 shows what DMorf's screen looks like when you first start it up.

HOW TO USE THE WIDGETS

See all of those buttons, check boxes, and other assorted gizmos in the windows in the bottom part of the screen? These are the graphic user interface control objects, known collectively as *widgets*, which you can use to tell

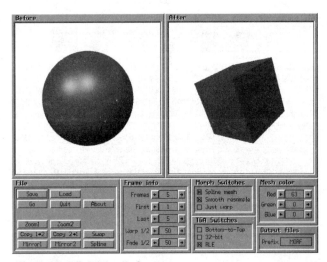

Figure 5-52 DMorf's Screen

DMorf what to do. There are three ways to activate a widget:

1. Click the mouse button while the cursor is pointing at the control.

2. If a particular control has a highlighted letter in its label, then you could also press the corresponding key on your keyboard.

3. Move the highlighted selection box to the widget of your choice, and press the space key.

Each of the different kinds of widgets will behave differently upon activation:

-   Activating a button will execute a command.

-   Activating a check box will toggle a setting.

-   If you click on the middle part of a number box, DMorf will clear the number in the box, give you a text cursor, and allow you to type in a new value. If you click on the little left arrow or right arrow buttons, DMorf will increment the number.

-   If you activate a text box, DMorf will clear the text in the box, present you with a text cursor, and allow you to type in a new value.

MORPHING WITH DMORF

Tell DMorf to perform the morph by clicking your mouse button on the "Go" button. DMorf will create as many new TGA files as were specified in the "Frames" number box. Because the default value for "Frames" is five, you'll get five files. This takes a while, so DMorf will display a status window (as shown in Figure 5-53).

```
Message
Processing frame 1 of 5...
Warping (first picture) row 30
```

Figure 5-53 Status Window

Figure 5-54 A Simple Fade

When DMorf is done, you'll have a series of TGA files, starting with MORF0001.TGA and ending with MORF0005. Figure 5-54 displays each of the intermediate pictures. The results are rather disappointing. The picture fades from one picture to the next, but the edges of the objects do not move. To get that kind of effect, you'll need to create a control mesh.

CREATING A CONTROL MESH

A control mesh is a series of horizontal lines that you superimpose over the pictures. You can move the intersection points around with your mouse to make the lines follow the contours of your objects. When DMorf morphs your pictures, it will warp them so that the contours match. You can add a vertical line to the pictures by placing the mouse cursor on the top or bottom border of one of the pictures at the point where you want the line to go, and clicking the right mouse button. Figure 5-55 shows the effect.

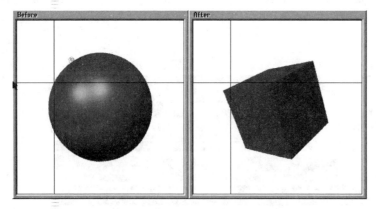

Figure 5-55 Adding a Vertical Line to the Mesh

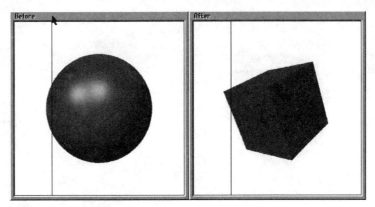

Figure 5-56 Adding a Horizontal Line to the Mesh

You can insert a horizontal line by clicking the mouse button while the cursor is in the left or right border of one of the pictures. Figure 5-56 shows the result.

Add enough horizontal and vertical lines to the mesh to cover the important features of each picture. You can change the location of an intersection by placing the mouse cursor near it and pressing and holding down the left mouse button. Move the mouse around until the intersection is where you want it, and then release the mouse button. Move the intersections in both of the pictures so that they identify the features. Figure 5-57 shows you what the resulting mesh should look like.

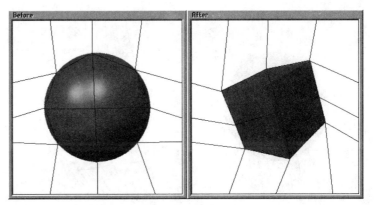

Figure 5-57 A Simple Control Mesh

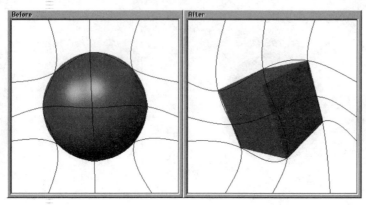

Figure 5-58 Spline View

We're not quite done, yet. DMorf doesn't actually use the lines that are displayed on the screen to warp the pictures. It warps using curved lines connecting the mesh intersections, creating a much more realistic effect. You can click on the "Spline" button to make DMorf display these curved lines instead of the straight line segments that it usually displays. For as long as you keep the mouse button pressed, DMorf will display a view much like Figure 5-58 .

The curves don't quite line up very well with the box picture, so we'll have to exert stronger control over our mesh. Figure 5-59 displays a mesh with a bunch of additonal lines added, and Figure 5-60 shows a spline view of the same mesh. The extra lines outside of the objects prevent strange curves at the points where the lines meet the edges of the objects.

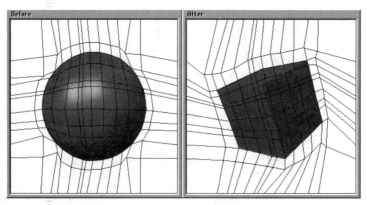

Figure 5-59 Tighter Control

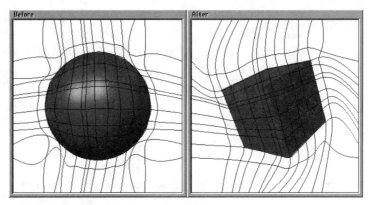

Figure 5-60 The Final Spline View

Click on the "Go" button again to test the actual morph. Figure 5-61 shows the intermediate pictures that DMorf will generate from that control mesh. Much better, isn't it?

Now would be a good time to save your work, if you haven't done so already. Click on the Save button, and DMorf will prompt you for a file name. Type in a name for your mesh. If you don't include a file extension, DMorf will tack a .MSH on to the end. Remember what the file name is, because the Load command doesn't display a list of existing mesh files.

BUILDING A FLIC

Time to compile all these TGA files into a flic so you can see how the morph looks when it's moving in real time. DMorf doesn't create copies of the original pictures, so remember to include them in the flic:

```
C:\> dta sphere.tga morf*.tga box.tga /p /osphbox
```

Figure 5-61 Final Morph Sequence

The /P parameter tells DTA to create a ping-pong effect, adding each picture to the flic a second time, in reverse order. So the resulting flic will contain frames in the order 0-1-2-3-4-5-4-3-2-1. The /O parameter tells DTA to name the flic SPHBOX.FLI.

If, as in this case, the two pictures are larger than 320x200 pixels, then you'll have to add a /R parameter to the DTA command. /R6 will tell DTA to create a 640x480 flic. You'll also have to use the DTAX command, because 640x480 flics use too much memory for DTA.EXE to handle. To create a high-resolution .FLC file, type

```
C:\> dtax sphere.tga morf*.tga box.tga /p /osphbox /r6
```

DISPLAYING THE FLIC

Run the Trilobyte flic player with this command:

```
C:\> play sphbox.fli
```

> or

```
C:\> play sphbox.flc
```

depending on whether you created a low- or high-resolution flic.

THE DMORF WIDGETS

The File panel, displayed in Figure 5-62, is a set of button widgets for saving and loading files, displaying copyright information, and manipulating your meshes. The buttons are

Load Loads a control file. Type the file name right the first time or you'll get a run-time error and get dumped out to DOS.

Save Saves your meshes and settings to a control file.

Go Causes DMorf to start morphing.

Quit Exits DMorf. The (ESC) key does the same thing.

About Displays a window containing program version information and copyright information.

Zoom1 and Zoom2 Displays just one of the images, much larger. This gives much finer control over the mesh points.

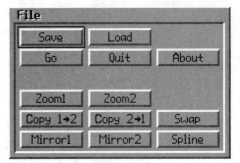

Figure 5-62 The File Panel

Copy 1 2 Copies the mesh from window 1 into window 2.

Copy 2 1 Copies the mesh from window 2 into window 1.

Mirror 1 Flips the mesh in window 1 horizontally.

Mirror 2 Flips the mesh in window 2 horizontally.

Swap Swaps the meshes between the two windows.

Splines: Gives you a preview of what splines for the current mesh points would look like. If you're using "Spline meshes" mode (explained in the next section), make sure you use this button once in a while to make sure the splines aren't going nuts.

The Frame Info panel, displayed in Figure 5-63, is a set of number box widgets that control animation settings. These widgets are

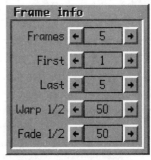

Figure 5-63 The Frame
Info Panel

Frames Tells DMorf how many pictures to create. If you're in Morph mode (explained in the next section), then this represents how many in-between frames to create. In warp mode, this number includes a fully warped final frame.

First and Last If you don't want to create a complete set of TGA files, you can use these controls to specify a range of output frames to generate.

The output range feature can be useful if you want to create morphs of animated sequences. Say, for example, you've got two 30-frame animations. For the first frame of the morph, load the first picture from each animation into DMorf. Create a mesh, set Frames to 30, set both First and Last to 1, and press the "Go" button. DMorf will generate a single output frame, MORF0001.TGA. Save the mesh in a file. Quit DMorf and start it up again, this time loading the second picture from each frame. Load and modify the mesh, set First and Last to 2, and press " Go." DMorf will create MORF0002.TGA. Repeat this 28 more times.

Warp 1/2 Change the rate at which DMorf warps the images. If you set Warp 1/2 to 75, then at 75% of the way through the morph the objects will only be half warped. The warp speeds up at that point so it finishes by the end of the morph.

Fade 1/2 Works the same as Warp 1/2, but affects the rate of the fade from the first picture to the second.

The Morph Switches panel, displayed in Figure 5-64, is a set of check-box widgets that control morph settings. These widgets are

Spline meshes When your points are all located where you want them to be, and you tell DMorf to go ahead and morph, DMorf figures out where to move each pixel by drawing spine curves between the vertices. If you turn this control off, it'll draw straight lines instead. Splined meshes almost always look much better, but you might want to use lines if (a) your splines go haywire, with curves going every which way, overlapping, sometimes even passing beyond the picture borders, and you don't feel like fixing it, or (b) you don't want something curved when it warps, or (c) you're in a rush, because lines are faster than splines.

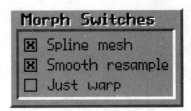

Figure 5-64 The Morph Settings Panel

Just Warp In the default mode, DMorf will map points from picture #1 toward picture #2, and from 2 toward 1, and cross-fade. In Warp mode, it'll just map points from #1 toward #2, with no fade. Not too surprisingly, Warp mode takes half the time that Morph mode does. You can use Just Warp as a quick and dirty method for moving an object across the screen without having to raytrace all of the frames.

Smooth resampling In Smooth mode, DMorf interpolates new pixel values from all source pixels. If you turn this control off, it will operate in Chunky mode, instead, and just grab the nearest pixel. Chunky mode is useful only for test runs, because it's much faster than Smooth mode, but it looks terrible.

The TGA Switches panel, displayed in Figure 5-65, is a set of check-box widgets that control the format of TGA files. These widgets are

RLE Tells DMorf whether or not to create run-length encoded (compressed) TGA files. Compressed TGA files are almost always smaller than non-compressed, but some programs can't read them. (DTA can).

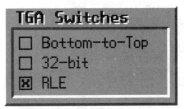

Figure 5-65 The TGA Settings Panel

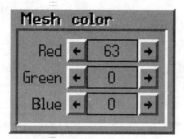

Figure 5-66 The Mesh Color Panel

32-Bit Tells DMorf whether to create 24-bit or 32-bit TGA files. The only reason you might want to use 32-bit TGA files is if you're planning to do compositing. Some programs can read only 24-bit TGA files. DTA can read either variety.

Bottom-to-Top Tells DMorf whether to create TGA files that begin at the bottom of the screen, or at the top of the screen. Some programs can only read one or the other variety. DTA can read either, but prefers the top-to-bottom variety.

The Mesh Color panel, displayed in Figure 5-66, is a set of number-box widgets that let you change the color of the mesh on your screen. This is useful if your meshes don't show up very well because of the shades of gray in your pictures. The default color, <63,0,0>, is a bright red color. You can change the red, green, and blue components of the color to any value from 0 to 63.

When DMorf creates TGA files, it begins the output file name with the prefix MORF, and adds a frame number to that. In Just Warp mode, DMorf uses WARP as the prefix instead. The Output Files panel, shown in Figure 5-67, contains a text box that allows you to change this prefix to any other four-letter word. Be polite.

Figure 5-67 The Output Files Panel

6 THE MOVIE PAGES

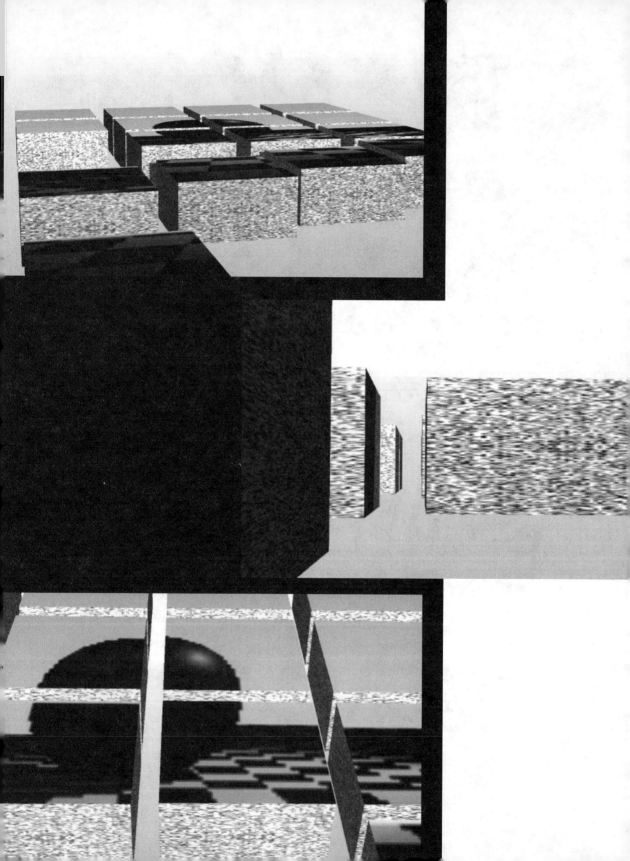

6 THE MOVIE PAGES

This chapter presents a series of completed animations. For each of these animations, we will explore how they are modeled and any motion and texture tricks that were used. Following the description of the animations, there are some brief suggestions of improvements or variations.

On the demonstration disk there is a separate directory for each one. The directory contains all of the data files required to create it, as well as a low-resolution sample flic.

ROCKET TAKEOFF

This scene opens on empty space. A tiny planet appears near the top of the screen. The camera zooms in on the planet, and soon the surface is all we can see. You notice a tiny rocket ship on the ground, so you keep zooming in until the rocket can be seen clearly. The rocket ship's engine ignites, and it blasts off into space. The rocket disappears in the distance. Suddenly, zoom! The rocket ship blasts back onto the screen from another direction, zips around in a loop, and careens off the screen, just missing you. Figure 6-1 shows selected frames from the animation.

DISCUSSION

Pieces of the data files appear in the following sections. The full data files can be found in the movie archives.

The Rocket

The rocket ship is built with shapes cut apart and glued together using Constructive Solid Geometry. The most common building block is a shape called

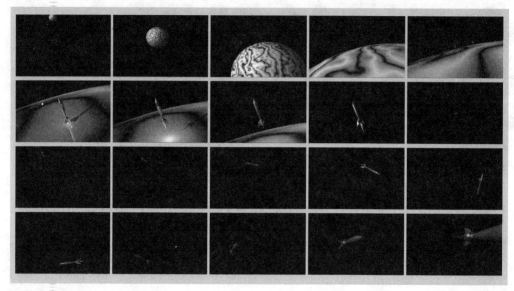

Figure 6-1 Rocket Takeoff Animation

a *piriform*. A piriform, shown in Figure 6-2, is a polynomial shape described with the equation $(x^4 - x^3) + y^2 + z^2$, which looks a lot like a teardrop or a Hershey's kiss.

The rocket cone is a squat piriform with the tip pointed up and the bottom shaved off. The neck of the rocket is a stretched piriform with the tip pointed down and both the top and bottom removed. The engine bulge is another short piriform, with the tip pointed downward and chopped off. Just add some tail fins carved out of spheres, and you have a 1950s science fiction movie rocket ship. Figure 6-3 shows each of these components, by itself and assembled.

Figure 6-2 A Piriform Object

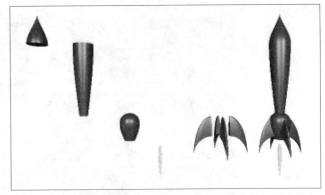

Figure 6-3 The Pieces that Make Up the Rocket Ship

Movement

Takeoff is really two separate animations pasted together into a single flic. The two portions show off some different methods for moving a rocket ship about.

In Part 1, all of the movement is created using equations based on velocity and acceleration. Take a look at LAUNCH.PI to see the details.

In Part 2, the curved path and acceleration are simulated using a spline path created with the SP program. Take a look at SPIN.BAT, SPIN.PI, and SPIN.PTH for the details.

SUGGESTED TWEAKS

Try some of the following to make your rocket takeoff animation more interesting:

- Improve the scenery. A starry sky would be nice, as would some authentic-looking craters on the surface of the planetoid.

- Supply some action! This scene could use some laser blasts, explosions, photon torpedos, and force fields.

- Add some kind of smoke effect to the takeoff. A torus makes a nice smoke ring.

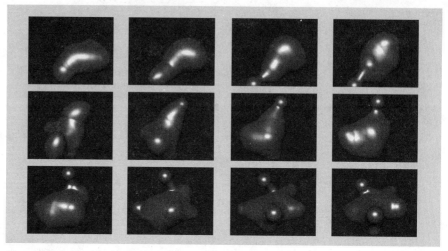

Figure 6-4 The Squirming Blob Animation

SQUIRMING BLOB

An oozing, squishy shape pulsates and writhes. Blob surfaces can be used to model very organic-looking objects by describing the locations and sizes of individual components. Polyray takes this description and smoothly connects the components to make a single object.

This animation moves the positions of a number of spherical blob components along circular and straight line paths so the resulting surface gives the impression of a single, squirming amoeboid shape. Figure 6-4 shows a sequence of frames from the animation.

DISCUSSION

The data file appears below, with some portions removed. For the full file, see SQUIRM.PI in the movie archives. The bulk of the file is composed of statements that set up the motion of the individual components of the blob. Each component will either follow a circular path, or bounce back and forth along a line segment. The rates at which the components orbit around, as well as the sizes of the circles they travel along, are defined in Listing 6-1.

LISTING 6-1 SQUIRM.PI

```
// Define the range of the animation
start_frame  0
end_frame    119
```

170

```
total_frames 120
outfile sqrm

// Give the (time dependent) location of the blob points
define ang radians(6 * frame)
define squirm_thresh 0.15

// The values of r and s are used to define how far each of the pieces of the
// blob move and how fast they move respectively.
define r10 1
define r11 1
define r20 2
define r21 1
...

define s1 3
define s2 2
define s3 1.5
define s4 1
...

// Define some offset angles - this way the blob pieces won't all be lined
// up when the animation starts.
define o09 radians(0)
define o10 radians(192)
define o11 radians(15)
...

//
// Define the positions of the various component parts of the blob, using
// the values defined above.  We have each of the 16 blob components moving in
// independent circles, ellipses, and lines.
//
define loc1 < r10 * cos(s1*ang), 0, r11 * sin(s1*ang)>
define loc2 < r20 * cos(s2*ang), 0, r21 * sin(s2*ang)>
...

define loc15 <r15x*cos(s15*ang+o15),r15y*cos(s15*ang+o15),r15z*cos(s15*ang+o15)>
define loc16 <r16x*cos(s16*ang+o16),r16y*cos(s16*ang+o16),r16z*cos(s16*ang+o16)>

// And finally we build the blob shape.
object {
   blob squirm_thresh:
      0.2, 3.0, loc1,
      0.2, 3.0, loc2,
      0.2, 3.0, loc3,
...
      0.2, 3.0, loc15,
      0.2, 3.0, loc16
   u_steps 20
   v_steps 20
   shiny_red
      }
```

SUGGESTED TWEAKS

This animation is built to loop over the course of 120 frames. Using a fixed number of frames in an animation is a drawback. We must be careful to use values for the movement of the blob components that will correctly loop after 120 frames. For exercise, change this data file so the number of frames can be altered. Refer to the use of `increment` in Chapter 4, *Advanced Techniques,* for examples of how that can be done.

Using blob primitives to build models is very different from using traditional primitives like spheres and cylinders. The drawback to using blobs is that they never seem to work quite like we expect—the exact location of the surface is very hard to predict. The advantage to blobs is that for certain types of models they work very well.

Blobs should be considered for effects that involve fluid, squishy, sorts of movements and objects. A few things that come to mind as candidates are drips from a faucet, bubbling oatmeal in a kettle, or alien blood floating in zero gravity. Here are a couple of project suggestions that could use blobs to advantage:

- Build a candle using cylindrical and spherical blob components. A blob would work very well for representing the wax. The body of the candle could be a cylindrical blob component. Add a flame to the top of the candle, perhaps using the flame example in Chapter 4, *Advanced Techniques,* as a guide. To simulate melting wax, move spherical blob components from the top of the candle down the sides.

- Build a fountain out of standard primitives, then move spherical blob components on parabolic paths out of the top of the fountain. A pool can be created at the base of the fountain by using a planar blob component and CSG.

SAUCER MORPH

A flying saucer zooms in from the left edge of the screen. When it hits the middle of the screen, it morphs into a rocket ship. The rocket flies off the top of the screen, then flies back on from the bottom. It turns back into a flying saucer and zooms off the right edge of the screen. Figure 6-5 shows selected frames from the animation.

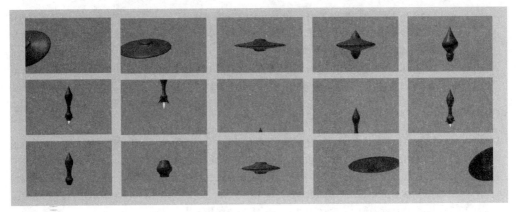

Figure 6-5 Saucer Morph Animation

DISCUSSION

As you could probably tell, this rocket shape is defined very differently from the one in the Takeoff flic. Here, instead of piecing the thing together with piriform shapes, the whole body is a single lathed object. Lathed objects are very flexible, allowing you to perform cool morphs. This is all it takes to define a flying saucer:

```
object {
   lathe 2, <0, 1, 0>, 7, <0,-2>, <2,-2>, <2,-1>, <10,0>, <2,1>, <2,2>, <0,2>
   bluesteel
}
```

The Polyray data file SAUCER.PI generates the whole animation. This discussion will not list every line, only highlights, so check out SAUCER.PI in the example files if you want to see the whole thing.

Saucer is divided into six steps with these equations:

```
define segmentsize (total_frames/6)
define segment floor(frame/segmentsize)
define percent1 (fmod(frame,segmentsize)/segmentsize)
```

These lines set two important variables, `segment`, which specifies which of the six segments the current frame is in, and `percent1`, a number between 0 and 1 that represents how far along the current frame is in that segment.

These variables determine every movement in the animation. The segment number determines which objects and numbers get moved, and the percentage determines how far to move them.

You can move an object using a simple equation, which will from now on be known as the in-between (or *tween*) equation:

```
define inbetween start + ((end-start)*percent1)
```

where start and end are either numbers or 3-D coordinates. The result is a new number or coordinate that varies between the start value and the end value in the same proportion that percent1 varies between 0 and 1. If percent1 is 0.25, then inbetween will be set to a number or coordinate exactly one-quarter of the way between start and end.

In the first step of this animation, the flying saucer moves from coordinate <–22,0,0> to <0,0,0>. The tween equation for this movement would be

```
define xloc -22+((0-(-22))*percent1)
```

or, simplified:

```
define xloc -22+(22*percent1)
```

To actually move the saucer object, you would just use the variable xloc in a translate statement. In the same manner, change the saucer's rotation about the *x*-axis from –90 to 0:

```
if { segment==0) {
  define xrot -90+(90*percent1)
  define yrot 0
}
elseif (segment==1) {
...
```

Also set the yrot variable, because even though Y rotation doesn't change in segment 0, it might in one of the other steps.

Because percent1 varies between 0 and 1 at a constant rate, all objects using that variable will have to move at a constant rate. That's fine for the first segment, because flying saucers move at a constant rate. It's not fine for the third segment, in which the rocket ship must blast off, because rocket ships don't. After the engine flames on, a rocket slowly starts moving, building up speed as it goes. Fortunately, there's a convenient (though arcane) equation that can help:

```
define newpercent 1-((2*(percent1^3))-(3*)percent1^2))+1)^power
```

This equation translates the percentage value from one number between 0 and 1 to a different number between 0 and 1. Depending on the value of power, the resulting number will be weighted closer to either 0 or 1. If power is set to 2, output values will be weighted closer to 1. The percentage 0.25 translates to about 0.28, 0.5 translates to 0.75, 0.75 translates to just a bit lower than 1, and 0 and 1 remain the same.

If power is set to 0.4151, then values are weighted closer to 0 by about the same amount. 0.25 translates to a number very close to 0, 0.5 translates to 0.25, and 0.75 translates to 0.5. Again, 0 and 1 stay the same. Near the top of SAUCER.PI, you'll find two versions of this equation, each with a different power value:

```
define percent2 1-((2*(percent1^3))-(3*(percent1^2))+1)^2
define percent3 1-((2*(percent1^3))-(3*(percent1^2))+1)^0.4151
```

So we now have three percentage values that we can use in in-betweening calculations. If we use percent1, an object will move at a constant rate. If we use percent2, an object will start moving slowly, and speed up as it reaches the end of the movement. If we use percent3, the object will start quickly and slow down until it reaches a stop.

SAUCER.PI uses percent2 to accelerate the rocket ship, and percent3 to slow it down as it returns from below the screen. Using the tweening equations and these nonlinear multipliers, morphing from a saucer to a rocket and back is simple. Just make sure that each object has the same number of control points, and tween between the control point coordinates of one object and the other. In SAUCER.PI, each control point is defined with a variable:

```
define saucer1 <0,-2>
define saucer2 <2,-2>
define saucer3 <2,-1>
define saucer4 <10,0>
define saucer5 <2,1>
define saucer6 <2,2>
define saucer7 <0,2>

define rocket1 <0.7,-6.5>
```

continued on next page

continued from previous page

```
define rocket2 <1.5,-4.5>
define rocket3 <0.5,-3.5>
define rocket4 <0.5,-0.5>
define rocket5 <1.5,2.5>
define rocket6 <0.6,4.5>
define rocket7 <0,6.5>
```

If the object is to remain a saucer for a whole segment, it uses the group of saucer variables to build a third set of variables:

```
if (object_ind==0) {
  define ctlpoint1 saucer1
  define ctlpoint2 saucer2
  define ctlpoint3 saucer3
  define ctlpoint4 saucer4
  define ctlpoint5 saucer5
  define ctlpoint6 saucer6
  define ctlpoint7 saucer7
}
```

If the object has to morph between a saucer and a rocket, it sets that same group of variables using the tweening equations:

```
else if (object_ind==1) {
  define ctlpoint1 saucer1+((rocket1-saucer1)*percent2)
  define ctlpoint2 saucer2+((rocket2-saucer2)*percent1)
  define ctlpoint3 saucer3+((rocket3-saucer3)*percent1)
  define ctlpoint4 saucer4+((rocket4-saucer4)*percent3)
  define ctlpoint5 saucer5+((rocket5-saucer5)*percent1)
  define ctlpoint6 saucer6+((rocket6-saucer6)*percent1)
  define ctlpoint7 saucer7+((rocket7-saucer7)*percent2)
}
```

Notice that the first and last points are tweened using `percent2`, so they start moving more quickly than the others; and the middle point uses `percent3`, so it moves more slowly than all of the other points. Later in the SAUCER.PI data file, these control point variables are used to build the surface of revolution:

```
object {
 lathe 2, <0, 1, 0>, 7,
 ctlpoint1,
 ctlpoint2,
 ctlpoint3,
 ctlpoint4,
 ctlpoint5,
 ctlpoint6,
 ctlpoint7
```

```
u_steps 64
bluesteel
rotate <xrot,0,0>
translate <xloc,yloc,0>
}
```

SUGGESTED TWEAKS

Here are more ideas for experimenting with morphing and movement:

- 🎬 Try morphing different shapes. There are many objects other than spacecraft that can be modeled with a surface of revolution — including vases, bottles, chess pieces, and light bulbs.

- 🎬 Experiment with different values of `power`, to make objects move at different rates.

PLANE ANIMATION

This animation demonstrates the use of connected spline paths. We will move a plane over a figure-eight course by connecting a set of four cubic splines. In addition to moving the plane along a path, we will also bank the plane back and forth as it makes its turns. A sequence of frames from the animation is shown in Figure 6-6.

Figure 6-6 The Airplane Animation

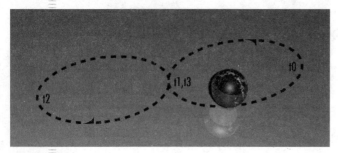

Figure 6-7 A Figure-Eight Course as a Series of Four Splines

DISCUSSION

As promised in Chapter 4, *Advanced Techniques,* we will connect a set of splines to make a complex path. The path here is a figure-eight course that we will fly a plane along. We want to simulate changes in position, changes in velocity, and changes in the bank of the plane. We can simultaneously generate all the in-between values for each of these from just a few values. The four curves that make up the course are shown connected together in Figure 6-7. The starting and ending key times in the figure correspond with the ends of the four spline curves.

First we define the key frames where things start and end. Because we are interested in keeping a consistent motion over the individual parts of the figure-eight course, the key frames are split into even quarters. The declarations to do this are shown in the following code (along with a variable `segment` that defines the one of the four splines we are currently following).

```
define start_times [0, total_frames/4, total_frames/2, 3*total_frames/4]
define end_times [total_frames/4, total_frames/2,
                    3*total_frames/4, total_frames]
define segment floor(4 * frame / total_frames)
```

The starting and ending key frames are placed into the variables `t0` and `t1` for use in later parts of the data file. These values have exactly the same role they did when we followed straight line and splined paths in Chapter 4, *Advanced Techniques.*

```
define t0 start_times[segment]
define t1 end_times[segment]
```

As usual, we need some way of generating the in-between frames. The variable `increment` tells us how far along we are on an individual spline path. For each of the four splines, the value of `increment` will vary from 0 at the start of the spline to 1 at the end of the spline.

```
//
// Figure out how far along we are in the animation
//
define increment (frame - t0) / (t1 - t0)
```

Now that the housekeeping is out of the way, let's define how the splines are connected together. There are four control points to the motion. There is a control point at each end of the figure-eight, and two in the very middle. The two points in the middle coincide in position; however, the velocities at these two points are exactly opposite.

```
//
// Define some values for the movement
//
define start_positions [<-10, 5, 0>, <0, 5, 0>, <10, 5, 0>, <0, 5, 0>]
define end_positions [<0, 5, 0>, <10, 5, 0>, <0, 5, 0>, <-10, 5, 0>]

define start_velocities [<0, 0, 10>, <20, 0, -20>, <0, 0, 10>, <-20, 0, -20>]
define end_velocities [<20, 0, -20>, <0, 0, 10>, <-20, 0, -20>, <0, 0, 10>]
```

The definitions of `pos0`, `pos1`, `vel0`, and `vel1` aren't strictly necessary. We could have used the actual indexed values of the position and velocity arrays instead. We do this just because it makes the calculation for the final position and velocity exactly the same as if we were working with a single spline rather than multiple ones.

```
define pos0 start_positions[segment]
define pos1 end_positions[segment]
define vel0 start_velocities[segment]
define vel1 end_velocities[segment]
```

Ick, math again! Well, the next few statements are what makes the cubic spline work. As long as we set things up consistently, using `increment` to determine the in-betweens, we can just cut and paste the following definitions of `u`, `u2`, etc. from data file to data file.

```
//
// Calculate the various coefficients of the spline path
//
define u   increment
define u2 (u * u)
define u3 (u2 * u)
define a0 (2 * u3 - 3 * u2 + 1)
```

continued on next page

continued from previous page

```
define a1 (-2 * u3 + 3 * u2)
define a2 (u3 - 2 * u2 + u)
define a3 (u3 - u2)
//
// Finally the position is calculated from the coefficients:
//
define pos (a0 * pos0 + a1 * pos1 + a2 * vel0 + a3 * vel1)
```

Now that the positioning is taken care of, let's get the airplane oriented. We do this by looking at how the velocity (remember velocity has direction as well as magnitude) changes from one key frame to another. A couple of simple calculations give us `norm_vel`, which is where the plane should be pointed. A couple more calculations and we can figure how to orient the plane along the direction of `norm_vel`.

```
//
// Now move the object
//
define increment_vel (a0 * vel0 + a1 * vel1)
define norm_vel increment_vel / fabs(increment_vel)
define half_angle (norm_vel + <1, 0, 0>) / 2
```

The next statement might look a bit odd, but there is a "gotcha" involved in calculating the value of `half_angle`. If the ending orientation is exactly opposite to the starting orientation, the value of `half_angle` will end up as <0,0,0>. This is bad. To cover this case, we check the length of `half_angle`. If it is too small, we know the bad case happened and something needs to be done. To fix it, we simply make an angle that we know will work for the one nasty case. The next two statements perform this fix.

```
if (|half_angle| < 0.001)
   define half_angle <0, 0, 1>
```

Up to now, we have generated the values for position and for orientation only in 2-D. However, if you have ever watched a plane fly, you know that it rolls into and out of turns. To simulate this effect, we define bank angles (roll) for the plane at the ends of each spline.

```
define start_banks [-80, 0, 80, 0]
define end_banks [0, 80, 0, -80]

define bank0 start_banks[segment]
define bank1 end_banks[segment]

define bank_angle (a0 * bank0 + a1 * bank1)
```

180

Yes, all the calculations are done and we are ready to put the airplane into the scene. The include file contains a declaration of an airplane that is oriented along the *x*-axis. Given the orientation along *x*, we just rotate back and forth before orienting to the direction of norm_vel to get the correct bank angle. After all the orientations are done, we translate the plane to its final position.

```
//
// Rotate and move the plane into position
//
include "plane.inc"
fighter_plane {
    rotate <180, 0, 0>
    rotate <bank_angle, 0, 0>
    rotate half_angle, 180
    translate pos
    }
```

In order to make the animation a little more interesting, we will add some objects and background detail. First of all, an air race has to follow a course, so we will make the figure-eight go around two checkered poles.

The checkered poles are simple cylinders with mirrored spheres on top. (The animation will need to be rendered in SVGA resolution to see good reflections in the spheres.) The definitions for the cylinders place them right in the middle of the loops of the eight.

```
object {
    cylinder <-8, 0, 0>, <-8, 7, 0>, 0.3
    texture { checker matte_white, matte_black }
    }
object { sphere <-8, 7, 0>, 0.5 mirror }
object {
    cylinder <8, 0, 0>, <8, 7, 0>, 0.3
    texture { checker matte_white, matte_black }
    }
object { sphere <8, 7, 0>, 0.5 mirror }
```

Next, we have to make an outdoor setting, so we add sky and ground. The sky and ground are a huge sphere and disk, respectively. The sky is made to look a little more natural by adding a "cloud" texture. The clouds are a noise function applied to shades of white and transparency. The ground is a tan color with ripples added so that it doesn't look too flat (perhaps we are in the desert and there are small dunes of sand). These textures, along with the definition of the airplane object, can be found in the file plane.inc.

```
// Add a cloudy sky to the picture
object {
    sphere <0, 0, 0>, 10000
    scale <1, 0.02, 1>
    cloudy_sky { scale <500, 500, 500> }
    }

// Define the desert floor
object {
    disc <0, 0, 0>, <0, 1, 0>, 10001
    ground_ripple { scale <100, 100, 100> }
    }
```

SUGGESTED TWEAKS

Where can we go from here? Well there are lots of things you can do with this animation. A race needs contenders, so add more airplanes and have them follow slightly different paths and move at slightly different speeds. Make the course more complex by adding more spline paths, perhaps varying the speeds over different parts of the course. For a video game effect, the viewpoint can be put at the front of a plane as it flies through the course....

The use of splines in animation is pervasive. If you can work through this example, you are well on the way to making your own complex paths. Start with simple paths like this one and build from there. As you accumulate data files, assembling the pieces starts to become easier and easier.

RUNNER

A shiny metal, human-shaped robot, named Polyman, runs across the screen. His gait is more amusing than it is authentic. Half of the fun in watching this

Figure 6-8 The Running Polyman

flic (at least in the high-resolution version) is watching the reflections on the ground and on his body. Figure 6-8 shows Polyman in action.

DISCUSSION

The movements in Runner operate much like the movements in the Saucer Morph animation. Over the course of the whole animation, Polyman moves from a starting position of <0,8.35,0> to an ending position of <0,8.35,-30> using a variation of the tweening equation. The animation is divided into eight segments, consisting of one forward step with each foot.

RUNNER.PI uses two include files: MAN.INC, which defines the objects that make up Polyman's body; and RUN.INC, which sets the amount of bending that takes place between each limb. The real action takes place in RUN.INC. For each segment, in-betweening equations change the amount of bending for each of the moving limbs from a starting position to an ending position, and back again. The trick to getting Polyman to run is to select the best starting and ending positions.

SUGGESTED TWEAKS

For more fun with Polyman, try these ideas:

- Add nonlinear movement. All limb movement in Runner is linear, which is extremely unlifelike. In the real world, a knee doesn't bend at the same speed for the whole duration of a step. The same applies to all of the other joints and limbs in the body. If you're really patient, you could try changing all of the movements so they are nonlinear.

- Build Polyman a human-looking head, or some clothing.

- Add a banana peel to the scene, right in Polyman's path. The results could be spectacular if you get him to slip on it just right.

CREDITS

Runner is based on a brilliant Polyray data file by Will Wagner called "Polyman." Dave Mason added the running motion.

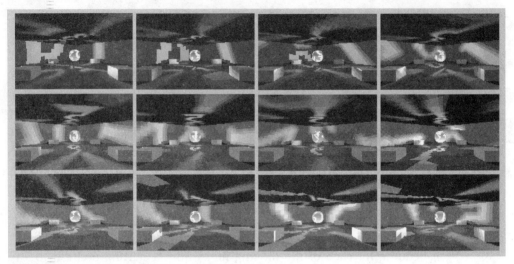

Figure 6-9 Environment-Mapped Disco Lights

DISCO LIGHT

Let's go back to the '70s! Here we are inside a room with a textured light source. By wrapping a set of images around a light source, it is possible to project these images outward to the walls of the room. This animation rotates the light about two separate axes, resulting in a lighting effect very reminiscent of the inside of a disco. A sequence of frames from the animation is shown in Figure 6-9.

DISCUSSION

Typically, environment maps are used to simulate reflections in renderings without using raytracing. Here we are going to turn the process around and project light outwards through the environment map. An environment map is a set of six images that are wrapped around a cube. Figure 6-10 shows the way the mapping works.

If you imagine image 2 staying where it is and the rest of the images wrapping around a cube, then you can see how the environment map is created. When it is used as a texture for a light source, the direction from the light source to an object is calculated and is used to determine a color from the appropriate part of the image map.

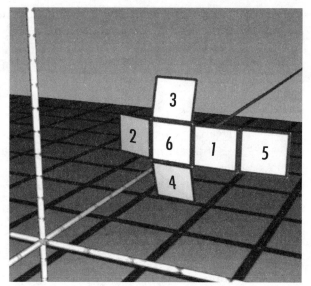

Figure 6-10 Placement of Images in an
Environment Map

The order of the images may seem a bit odd, but it works like this: 1 and 2 are the positive and negative *x* directions; 3 and 4 are the positive and negative *y* directions; and 5 and 6 are the positive and negative *z* directions. To use an environment map, you need a declaration that looks like this:

```
define block_environ
environment("one.tga", "two.tga", "three.tga",
            "four.tga", "five.tga", "six.tga")
```

Each of the strings names a particular image file. For the lighting animation, we declare a textured light source by making the environment map wrap around the location of the light. The simplest way to get the map positioned correctly around the light is to define the map at the origin, then translate it to where it should finally be. Note the rotation statement in the declaration—it revolves the light around, causing the projections of the images to sweep up and down the walls.

```
textured_light {
   color environment_map(P, block_environ)
   rotate <frame*6, frame*3, 0>
   translate <0, 2, 0>
   }
```

The complete text for this animation can be found in the file ILIGHT.PI in the movie archives. Notice that the images we used are very low resolution—because for a typical 320x200 resolution animation, using a high-resolution image is overkill. If you go to SVGA, the images should be of greater detail.

SUGGESTED TWEAKS

Suggestions for things to do with this animation include using different images (fractal images are pretty nice if you are willing to render your frames at high resolution), add more lights to make a really flashy disco, or play with different functions for the light sources (a textured light doesn't have to be an image, any vector function will do).

BOUNCING BALLS

Bounce shows six spheres bouncing up and down on a reflective plane. Because most folks who are not getting started in 3-D animation try a bouncing ball scene as an early project, this theme is overused. However, this one has a few interesting variations. If you look at one of the balls all by itself, you'll see it moves in a pretty authentic-looking bounce, slowing down as it moves up into the air, speeding up as it approaches the ground, and squishing when it hits. If you look at the whole group, you'll see that the balls form a sine-wave pattern. Figure 6-11 shows a preview of the flic.

Figure 6-11 Bouncing Balls

DISCUSSION

Each ball starts bouncing at a different point. The first ball starts in the first frame of the animation. The second starts one-sixth of the way through. The third, two-sixths of the way, and so on. We accomplish this by assigning each ball its own time value, like this:

```
define time1 frame
define time2 fmod(frame+((total_frames/6)*2,total)
define time3 fmod(frame+((total_frames/6)*3,total)
define time4 fmod(frame+((total_frames/6)*4,total)
define time5 fmod(frame+((total_frames/6)*5,total)
define time6 fmod(frame+((total_frames/6)*6,total)
```

Assuming a 60-frame animation, ball 2's time value will be set to 50 for frame 0, at 0 for frame 10, at 10 for frame 20, and so on. Each ball's height is based on this time value. We use a sine function to superficially simulate gravity. The ball moves quickly when it's close to the ground, and more slowly the higher it gets. The height function looks like this:

```
define height1 0.5+(sin(radians(time*(180/total_frames)))*5)
```

The balls each have a radius of 1, so if the lowest height a ball can reach is 0.5, then part of the sphere is going to be underground. We get around this by squishing the spheres just enough so that the bottom is in contact with the ground.

```
if (height1<1) {
  define vscale1 height1
  define hscale1 1+((1-height1)*2)
}
else {
  define vscale 1
  define vscale 2
}
```

With these values defined, all that's left to do is to place the sphere in position:

```
object {
  sphere <0,0,0>,1
  steel_blue
  scale <hscale1,vscale1,hscale1>
  translate <-7.5,height1,0>
}
```

The height value can be used in other ways, as well. In the second sphere, the color of the sphere is based on the height of the sphere. It starts out with a modified version of the equation from the first ball:

```
define height2a sin(radians(time2*(180/total_frames)))
define height2 0.5+(height2a*5)
```

The `height2` variable varies between 0.5 and 5.5, just like `height1`. `height2a`, however, varies between 0 and 1. This is perfect for color calculations, because each component (red, green, and blue) of an actual color is a number in that range.

```
object {
  sphere <0,0,0>,1
  texture {
    surface {
      color <1-height2a,0,height2a>
      ambient 0.1
      diffuse 0.5
      specular white, 0.7
      reflection white, 0.5
    }
  }
  scale <hscale2,vscale2,hscale2>
  translate <-4.5,height2,0>
}
```

When the sphere is at the top of its fall, this will result in a bright blue coloring. As it falls, the color fades to red.

SUGGESTED TWEAKS

Here are more possibilities for experimenting with bouncing objects:

- Try modifying a ball's movement to more accurately depict the interaction of physical forces, like gravity. In the real world, bouncing is much more complicated than a sine-wave function. An object begins falling with some initial velocity, and gets pulled toward the ground at 9.8 meters per second. How high it bounces back up is based on a combination of the speed it's traveling at when it hits and what material it's made of. It loses some height each time it bounces, until eventually it stops bouncing completely.

◀ Try bouncing some more interesting shapes, perhaps some odd blobby objects.

◀ The flic version on the disk, BOUNCE.FLI, was generated from BOUNCE.PI at 160x100 resolution, with only 30 frames. If you want to see it in all its glory, re-render it at 640x480, with 200 frames. It has to be raytraced, because of all the reflections.

SUPERQUADRIC MORPH

This animation shows a couple of useful techniques. The first is a way to smoothly morph between two shapes using superquadrics. The second shows how to generate an animation from a C program. Superquadrics are an incredibly versatile set of formulas that can be used to smoothly model transformations between spheres, boxes, octahedrons, etc. An external program is used to generate data files because the models you want to render are sometimes controlled better by a real programming language.

A set of C routines that can be used to generate data files is included in the Polyray data archives. These routines include calls for viewpoint creation, light declarations, and declarations for some of the more common shapes (including sphere, box, and cone). The library also supports multiple raytracers, so if there are features that don't exist in Polyray, you can use the same C code to generate data files for another raytracer.

The morph goes through the following shapes: sphere, pinchy, pinched cone, cylinder, cube, pillow, and back to sphere. Figure 6-12 shows a sequence of shapes from the sphere to the pinchy, to the pinched cone.

DISCUSSION

The program that generates this transformation is now outlined in detail. The code is from the program SUPERQ.C, and is included in the movie archives. The actual code is interspersed with comments describing what is going on.

The first thing to do is to define the viewpoint, lights, and background. The process is very similar to the one in Polyray. Each piece of the scene is created using C data structures, then the library code is used to generate the actual data file. Note that in this program we are using the Polyray format for the output; however, you could also use one of the other renderer output formats.

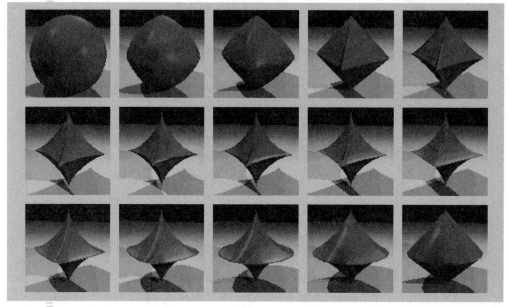

Figure 6-12 A Morphing Superquadric Shape

We put all the statements needed to generate the scene in the first procedure, `make_superq_file`. Following this procedure, we will see the sequences that generate the individual frames. This procedure gets called for every frame (we need to generate an entire data file for each frame). An alternative to this approach would be to generate the viewpoint and lights only once and save them in an include file. When generating the superquadric object, simply include the viewpoint file.

```
static void
make_superq_file(FILE *outfile, double pow1, double pow2)
{
    COORD4  back_color, obj_color;
    COORD4  backg[4], light;
    COORD4  from, at, up;
    COORD4  center_pt;
    double  lscale, radius, r0, r1;
    int  i;
```

After getting that nasty variable declaration business out of the way, we are ready to start doing things. First off, we tell the library what file to place the scene data into. Followed by that we define the renderer we are going to use so that the library will know how to format the scene file.

```
lib_set_output_file(outfile);
lib_set_raytracer(OUTPUT_POLYRAY);
lib_set_polygonalization(size_factor, size_factor);

/* set radius of sphere which would enclose entire object */
radius = 1.5;
```

Standard stuff here. We build a viewpoint using from, at, and up, very similarly to the way we used the Polyray declaration. The variables following these in the lib_output_viewpoint call define the field of view (angle in a Polyray file), the aspect ratio, the hither plane, and finally the resolution of the output image.

After defining the viewpoint, the next few statements set the background color, then set up three lights. The intensity of the lights is scaled so that the image won't get washed out. The brightness of lights is a value that needs a little bit of tweaking from raytracer to raytracer; so if you use something other than Polyray, you may want to increase or decrease the value of lscale.

```
/* output viewpoint */
SET_COORD(from, 1, 5.0, 1.5);
SET_COORD(at, 0.0, 0.0, 0.0);
SET_COORD(up, 0.0, 0.0, 1.0);
lib_output_viewpoint(&from, &at, &up, 45.0, 1.0, 0.01, 128, 128);

SET_COORD(back_color, 0.0, 0.0, 0.0);
lib_output_background_color(&back_color);

/* output light sources */
lscale = 1.0 / sqrt(3.0);
SET_COORD4(light, 4.0, 3.0, 2.0, lscale);
lib_output_light(&light);
SET_COORD4(light, 1.0, -4.0, 4.0, lscale);
lib_output_light(&light);
SET_COORD4(light, -3.0, 1.0, 5.0, lscale);
lib_output_light(&light);

/* output floor polygon - beige */
SET_COORD(back_color, 1.0, 0.75, 0.33);
lib_output_color(&back_color, 0.2, 0.8, 0.0, 0.0, 0.0, 0.0, 1.0);
r0 = radius * 20.0;
r1 = -radius;
```

continued on next page

continued from previous page

```
SET_COORD(backg[0],   r0,   r0,  r1);
SET_COORD(backg[1],  -r0,   r0,  r1);
SET_COORD(backg[2],  -r0,  -r0,  r1);
SET_COORD(backg[3],   r0,  -r0,  r1);
lib_output_polygon(4, backg);
```

Now we get to the good bit. The shape of the superquadric is determined by the value of pow1 and pow2. These values are passed in from the main driver, and by modulating them, we get the shape transformations. The color of the superquadric is set to a purple color, and the lighting characteristics are defined through the lib_output_color statement. (The values chosen give an ambient value of 0.2, diffuse of 0.7, specular highlights of 0.3, and a specular angle of 5 degrees.)

```
/* output superquadric at location defined by center */
SET_COORD(obj_color, 1.0, 0.5, 0.8);
SET_COORD4(center_pt, 0.0, 0.0, 0.0, 1.0);
lib_output_color(&obj_color, 0.2, 0.7, 0.0, 0.3, 5.0, 0.0, 1.0);
lib_output_sq_sphere(&center_pt, radius, radius, radius, pow1, pow2);
}
```

That's all there is to building a data file. What follows is the driver code. This code steps through various values for the shape parameters of a superquadric. After each file is generated by the preceding procedure, a call is made to Polyray to render the image. After all images have been rendered, we then call DTA to crunch them into an animation.

```
int
main(int argc, char *argv[])
{
    FILE *outfile;
    int i, cnt = 30;
    double power;
    char txt[64];
```

A superquadric is defined by two control values. They determine how round or how pinchy the superquadric will be. One controls the shape around its equator, the other controls its shape from north pole to south pole in an animation. A spherical shape is formed using the control values [1, 1]. A pinchy is formed from the values [3, 3]. The loop in the following code generates values that smoothly go from 1 to 3 over the course of cnt frames. By changing the value of cnt in the previous declaration, you can make the animation coarser or smoother.

The sequence of steps in each loop is

1.   Create the new control value(s).

2.   Open a file to hold the scene data.

3.   Generate the new control values.

4.   Generate the data file.

5.   Close the scene file.

6.   Render the data file.

7.   Change the name of the image to be correctly in sequence.

The values here are identical, so a single power value that varies from 1 to 3 is created. As it is generated, a call to make_superq_file is made. This results in a data file that is stored in SUPERQ.PI. The call to system is used to get Polyray to render the file.

```
/* First loop: turn from an sphere into an octagonal pinchy */
for (i=0;i<cnt;i++) {
    outfile = fopen("superq.pi", "w");
    power = 1.0 + 2.0 * (double)i / (double)cnt;
    make_superq_file(outfile, power, power);
    fclose(outfile);
    system("polyray superq.pi");
    sprintf(txt, "ren out.tga out%03d.tga", i);
    system(txt);
}
```

Second verse, same as the first. Here we vary only one of the two control values. The first control value is set to 3 for the entire sequence. The second varies from 3 down to 1. The generation of files and rendering is as shown in the previous code.

```
/* Second loop: turn from an octagonal pinchy into a pinched double cone */
for (i=0;i<cnt;i++) {
    outfile = fopen("superq.pi", "w");
    power = 3.0 - 2.0 * (double)i / (double)cnt;
    make_superq_file(outfile, 3.0, power);
    fclose(outfile);
    system("polyray superq.pi");
    sprintf(txt, "ren out.tga out%03d.tga", i + 30);
    system(txt);
}
```

There are three more loops like the previous ones, then finally we get to the transformation that takes us back to the sphere:

```
/* Sixth loop: turn from a pillow into a sphere */
for (i=0;i<cnt;i++) {
   outfile = fopen("superq.pi", "w");
   power = (double)i / (double)cnt;
   make_superq_file(outfile, 1.0, power);
   fclose(outfile);
   system("polyray superq.pi");
   sprintf(txt, "ren out.tga out%03d.tga", i + 150);
   system(txt);
   }
```

All the frames have been generated. All that is left to do is to use DTA to assemble the animation. Once that is done, we can remove the individual frames.

```
/* Now use DTA to assemble the animation */
system("dta out*.tga");

/* Finally, remove all the Targa files */
/*  system("del out*.tga"); */
}
```

SUGGESTED TWEAKS

Much of what you just saw is very similar to the techniques we used in Chapter 4, *Advanced Techniques*. The difference here is that we are able to use a set of C routines to generate an animation of a surface that is very slow to render as an implicit surface, but not too slow as polygonal patches. A big benefit of using this sort of approach is that the library code has been written to support several raytracers. You can use the very same code to generate data files and animations using something other than Polyray.

MAKING MOVIES LOGO

The first animation example in this book now becomes one of the last. The words "Making" and "Movies," carved out of shiny metal, rotate in opposite directions. It's not too eventful, but what good is a book on animation without at least one whirling logo? Figure 6-13 displays a preview of the logo animation.

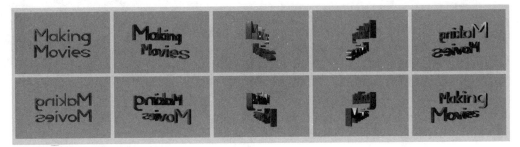

Figure 6-13 Whirling Logo

DISCUSSION

LOGO.PI is a short data file. Other than typical camera and light source information, this is all there is.

```
include "letters.inc"
// Place the letters for the word "Making"
object {
 capital_m
 + lowercase_a { translate <1.7,0,0 > }
 + lowercase_k { translate <3.15,0,0 > }
 + lowercase_i { translate <3.85,0,0 > }
 + lowercase_n { translate <4.85,0,0 > }
 + lowercase_g { translate <6.25,0,0 > }
 shiny_blue
 translate <-3,1.3,0>
 rotate <0,-rotation,0>
}
// place the letters for the word "Movies"
object {
 capital_m
 + lowercase_o { translate <1.7,0,0 > }
 + lowercase_v { translate <3,0,0 > }
 + lowercase_i { translate <3.925,0,0 > }
 + lowercase_e { translate <4.875,0,0 > }
 + lowercase_s { translate <6.2,0,0 > }
 shiny_blue
 translate <-3,-1.3,0>
 rotate <0,rotation,0>
}
```

Logo builds each word by laying down predefined objects for each of the letters in a row. Each letter is approximately 1 unit wide, but some are narrower and some are wider, so it requires some trial-and-error to get the letters correctly spaced. Each word constitutes a separate object, so you can translate it as a unit and rotate the whole word.

The real work is done in LETTERS.INC. Each letter is made up of combinations of cylinders and boxes. The lowercase letter "o" is the simplest in the repertoire:

```
define lowercase_o object {
 ( object { cylinder <0,-0.4,-2>,<0,-0.4,2>,0.6 } -
   object { cylinder <0,-0.4,-2>,<0,-0.4,2>,0.4 }
 ) *
 object { box <-1,0.3,-0.3>,<1,-1.1,0.3> }
```

The subtraction of one cylinder from another gives the "o" some thickness. The intersection with a box chops off the ends and provides a cap at each end. The lowercase "i" is just a box with a capped cylinder hovering above it. You should study each of the characters in LETTERS.PI. It's a good introduction to Constructive Solid Geometry.

SUGGESTED TWEAKS

Try the following variations on the Making Movies logo:

- Create your own logo. This will take some work, because LETTERS-.INC includes only enough of the alphabet to spell "Making Movies."

- Add some extra movement to the logo. It would look nice if, in addition to rotating words, individual letters rotated in various directions.

- Add some texture to the letters. Polyray can generate a wide variety of different surface characteristics, so you might as well use as many of them as you can. Try a different texture for each letter.

- You could just as easily perform tranformations other than rotation. Scaling has a lot of possibilities, or you could shear the letters to create italics.

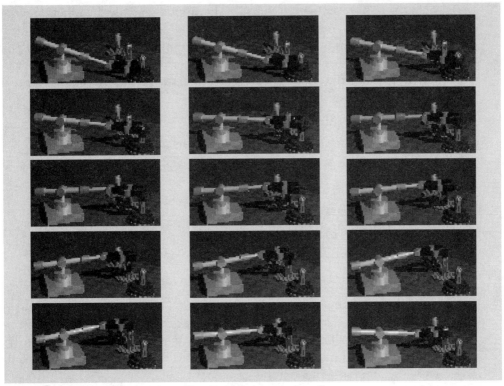

Figure 6-14 A Sequence from the Robot Arm Animation

ROBOT ARM

This animation is the most complex to use only Polyray to generate the frames. We will model a simple robot arm that plays the game "Towers of Hanoi." The object of the game is to move a set of wafers from one of three pegs to another peg. Only one wafer can be moved at a time, and it can only be moved on top of a disk that is wider than itself. The frames in Figure 6-14 show the robot arm as it moves a wafer from one peg to another.

DISCUSSION

When we get everything modeled, we will have an animation of a robot arm solving the game. There are two major components that need to be modeled: the disks and the robot arm. In addition, the ground and the pegs hold the wafers. During the course of the animation, only the wafers and the arm will move.

The animation is broken into a sequence of moves. Each move takes a wafer from one peg and moves it to another peg. It takes a total of seven moves to move the entire stack of three wafers. Each move is broken into a series of submoves. The submoves are

1. Grasp a wafer.

2. Move the wafer up off the peg it is on.

3. Move the wafer over to the peg it is going to.

4. Lower the wafer onto the new peg.

5. Ungrasp the wafer.

6. Raise the robot arm.

7. Move the robot arm to the peg that has the next wafer.

8. Lower the arm to a grasping position for the next peg.

Due to the complexity of this animation, a blow-by-blow description is not given. Instead, an overview is given of each of the data files that contributes to the animation. By reading through the data files and working out how the pieces fit together, the data from this animation can be adapted to reuse the robot arm in a number of ways.

There are five data files for this animation: ROBARM.PI, ROBTEX.INC, PEGS.INC, ROBWAFER.INC, and ROBARM.INC. Each of these files plays a very distinct part in building the animation. Each of the files and the role it plays is described below.

The file ROBARM.PI is the controlling file: it sets up the viewpoint, defines the number of frames that will be used for each sequence within the animation, and reads in the include files that build the models.

The file ROBTEX.INC builds definitions of the textures that will be used for the different objects. Chrome and brass are used for the robot arm, wood is used for the pegs, and jade is used for the wafers.

The file PEGS.INC builds the pegs. These pegs are a very simple combination of cylinders, disks, and a sphere. They have a wide circular base, a central pole, and a rounded top. The wood texture applied to each peg is translated and rotated so that the three pegs don't look like exact copies of each other. In addition, the base and center of each peg has the wood applied differently. This is to avoid the appearance that the entire peg was carved from a single piece of wood.

The file ROBWAFER.INC builds and places each of the wafers during the animation. The variables `submove` and `submove_increment` that are built in ROBARM.PI are used to build several new variables. These new variables define the locations of each of the three wafers, and set variables that determine how the arm needs to be oriented. The wafer positions are defined by `wafer_height0`, `wafer_height1`, `wafer_height2`, `wafer_offset0`, `wafer_offset1`, and `wafer_offset2`. The orientation of the arm is built from the variables `moving_wafer_offset`, `moving_wafer_height`, and `wafer_width`.

The file ROBARM.INC builds the robot arm and places it according to the values of the variables: `robarm_arm_alpha`, `robot_arm_beta`, `robot_arm_theta`, and `section2_offset`. `Robot_arm_alpha` swings the entire arm around its base. `Robot_arm_beta` moves the entire arm up and down. `Robot_arm_theta` opens and closes the fingers of the robot. `Section2_offset` defines how far out the extendable part of the arm is stretched. These four variables are all that are needed to control the movement and grasping of the robot arm.

SUGGESTED TWEAKS

This animation still has a couple of rough spots. The most noticeable is that the hand is opened to the size of the next disk immediately after placing the last one. This causes a visible problem if the next disk is smaller than the last. The fingers of the arm appear to go inside the last disk for a moment. To correct this, right after placing a disk, the hand should be opened wider than the largest disk. During the movement in the preceding steps 5 through 8, the hand should stay fully open. Only when the hand is in position to grasp the next disk should it close.

This animation takes quite a while to render. Running this animation in wireframe is a good way to preview what it will look like. The command to do this follows. On a fast machine (33Mhz 486 or faster), a frame will be displayed every couple of seconds.

```
C:> polyray robarm.pi -r 2
```

There are many ways to go from here. The uses of jointed figures manipulating objects is endless. Start by building new scenes that involve an arm manipulating objects. An animation of the arm picking up cylinders and boxes, then placing them into round and square holes, would be a good way to explore how one object manipulates another. To go one step beyond that, the robot arm could pick up cylinders and boxes that then change shape as the arm tries to put them into the wrong shaped hole.

APPENDIX A

Here it is, the end of the book already! And we've only scratched the surface. If you want to learn more, this appendix will point you in some likely directions.

ONLINE

Some of the best places to get up-to-date information on what people in the PC world are doing with rendering and computer animation are available through a telephone and a modem. In each of the following online services and bulletin board systems, you can usually find the latest and greatest versions of the software included with this book, and communicate with a lot of gung ho graphics fanatics:

- CompuServe Information System's GRAPHDEV forum. CIS can be expensive, but this is where things are happening. GRAPHDEV is also the home of FRACTINT and the Persistence of Vision raytracer (POV-Ray).

- You Can Call Me Ray BBS, a.k.a. YCCMR, (708) 358-5611. Located in Palatine, IL, owned and operated by Bill Minus. A classic bulletin board for graphics freaks.

- The Graphics Alternative BBS, a.k.a. TGA, (510) 524-2780. Located in El Cerito, CA, owned and operated by Adam Shiffman. This bulletin board has a wide variety of message areas covering different computer graphics topics, and an incredibly large collection of graphics and animation-related files. TGA is also the graphics hub for the Professional CAD and Graphics Network (PCG-Net).

GRAPHICS AND ANIMATION PROGRAMMING

A few books that the authors have found indispensible:

- *Computer Graphics: Principles and Practice* by Foley, Van Dam, Feiner, and Hughes (1990, Addison Wesley). This one is the bible of computer graphics programming. It covers about any graphics topic you can think of (however, occasionally it is a bit difficult to follow).

- *Advanced Animation and Rendering Techniques* by Alan Watt and Mark Watt (1992, Addison Wesley). This one's full of all sorts of cutting-edge stuff, and it's fun to read, too.

- The *Graphics Gems* series, Andrew Glassner, Senior Editor (Academic Press). There's a new one of these every year or two, and they're loaded with short articles on every graphics topic you can think of. There's plenty of C code included.

WIN $$

APPENDIX B

Waite Group Press is going Hollywood! Here's your chance to show off your knowledge of computer animation and dazzle us by using the programs in this book to create your own movie. You don't need a studio-sized budget, just your creativity, a spectacular viewpoint, and a little spirit of competition. We're looking for innovative, dramatic, state-of-the-art flics that show off the magic of the PC and simple ray-tracing software. Please keep the size of the movie under 1.44 MB so it fits on one 3.5" High Density disk. You could quickly be on the road to riches and fame.

To enter, mail your *original flic* and source code, with the entry card on the next page or a 3x5 postcard that includes your name, address, daytime phone number, the title of your entry, and a brief description of the movie.

RULES AND REGULATIONS

Eligibility: Your submission must be submitted betwen June 30 and October 31, 1993; it must be created with the Polyray program provided in this book; and the size of the flic must be under 1.44 MB, to fit on a single *high density* disk.

Dates and deadlines: Entries must be received at the address provided by 5PM, October 31,1993. Winners will be notified by March 31, 1994.

Preparation of entries: Only one flic may be submitted per entry, but you may enter as often as you like. Entries must be on a 3.5-inch disk and each disk must be labeled with your name, phone number, and the name of the flic. Waite Group Press is not responsible for lost or damaged entries. Waite Group Press will not return any entries unless entrants include a self-addressed stamped envelope designated for that purpose with their entry.

Judging and prizes: Flics will be judged on the basis of technique, creativity, and presentation by a panel of judges from Waite Group Press. Winners will be notified by March 31, 1994. For the names of the "Making Movies Film Festival" winners and his/her entry, send a self-addressed, stamped envelope, after April 15, 1994, to: Waite Group Press "Making Movies Film Festival," Contest Winner, 200 Tamal Plaza, Corte Madera, CA 94925.

Etc: No purchase necessary. Waite Group Press "Making Movies Film Festival" is subject to all federal, state, local, and provincial laws and regulations and is void where prohibited. Waite Group Press "Making Movies Film Festival" is not open to employees of The Waite Group, Inc., Publishers Group West, participating promotional agencies, any WGP distributors, and the families of any of the above. By entering the "Making Movies Film Festival," each contestant warrants that he or she is the original author of the work submitted, non-exclusively licenses The Waite Group, Inc. to duplicate, modify, and distribute the flic, and agrees to be bound by the above rules.

Name _____ Daytime Phone _____

Address _____

City _____ State _____ Zip _____

Entry (file name) _____

What should we know about this flic _____

_____

_____

_____

Send entries to: **"Making Movies Film Festival"**
Waite Group Press
200 Tamal Plaza
Corte Madera, CA 94925

I signify that the enclosed is my own original work and that I abide by all rules described in this Appendix B.

Signature _____

INDEX

Books have a substantial influence on the destruction of the forests of the Earth. For example, it takes 17 trees to produce one ton of paper. A first printing of 30,000 copies of a typical 480 page book consumes 108,000 pounds of paper which will require 918 trees!

Waite Group Press™ is against the clear-cutting of forests and supports reforestation of the Pacific Northwest of the United States and Canada, where most of this paper comes from. As a publisher with several hundred thousand books sold each year, we feel an obligation to give back to the planet. We will therefore support and contribute a percentage of our proceeds to organizations which seek to preserve the forests of planet Earth.

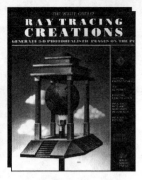

RAY TRACING CREATIONS

Drew Wells, Chris Young

With the **Ray Tracing Creations** book/disk combination, you can immediately begin rendering perfect graphic objects with ease. Using the powerful shareware program POV-RAY, you'll learn to control the location, shape, light, shading, and surface texture of all kinds of 3-D objects. POV-Ray's C-like language is used to describe simple objects, planes, spheres, and more complex polygons. Over 100 incredible pre-built scenes are included that can be generated, studied, and modified in any way you choose. This book provides a complete course in the fundamentals of ray tracing that will challenge and entice you. VGA display required.

ISBN: 1-878739-27-1, 600 pages, 1-5.25" disk and color plate section, $39.95, Available now

IMAGE LAB

Tim Wegner

This book is a complete PC-based "digital darkroom" that covers virtually all areas of graphic processing and manipulation. It comes with the finest graphics shareware available today: Piclab, CShow, Improces, Image Alchemy, and POV-Ray. This treasure chest of software lets you paint, draw, render and size images, remove colors, adjust palettes, combine, crop, transform, ray trace, and convert from one graphics file to another. Supercharged tutorials show how to make 3-D fractals and combine them to make photorealistic scenes. Plus, all the tools included have support forums on CompuServe so you can easily get the latest help and news.

ISBN: 1-878739-11-5, 459 pages, 1-3.5" disk and color poster, $39.95, Available now

WAITE GROUP PRESS™

This is a legal agreement between you, the end user and purchaser, and The Waite Group®, Inc., and the authors of the programs contained in the disk. By opening the sealed disk package, you are agreeing to be bound by the terms of this Agreement. If you do not agree with the terms of this Agreement, promptly return the unopened disk package and the accompanying items (including the related book and other written material) to the place you obtained them for a refund.

SOFTWARE LICENSE

1. The Waite Group, Inc. grants you the right to use one copy of the enclosed software programs (the programs) on a single computer system (whether a single CPU, part of a licensed network, or a terminal connected to a single CPU). Each concurrent user of the program must have exclusive use of the related Waite Group, Inc. written materials.

2. Each of the programs, including the copyrights in each program, is owned by the respective author and the copyright in the entire work is owned by The Waite Group, Inc. and they are therefore protected under the copyright laws of the United States and other nations, under international treaties. You may make only one copy of the disk containing the programs exclusively for backup or archival purposes, or you may transfer the programs to one hard disk drive, using the original for backup or archival purposes. You may make no other copies of the programs, and you may make no copies of all or any part of the related Waite Group, Inc. written materials.

3. You may not rent or lease the programs, but you may transfer ownership of the programs and related written materials (including any and all updates and earlier versions) if you keep no copies of either, and if you make sure the transferee agrees to the terms of this license.

4. You may not decompile, reverse engineer, disassemble, copy, create a derivative work, or otherwise use the programs except as stated in this Agreement.

GOVERNING LAW

This Agreement is governed by the laws of the State of California.

SATISFACTION REPORT CARD

Please fill out this card if you want to know of future updates to *Making Movies on Your PC,* or to receive our catalog.

Company Name: _____

Division/Department: _____   Mail Stop: _____

Last Name: _____   First Name: _____   Middle Initial: _____

Street Address: _____

City: _____   State: _____   Zip: _____

Daytime telephone: (_____)_____

Date product was acquired: Month _____ Day _____ Year _____   Your Occupation: _____

Overall, how would you rate *Making Movies on Your PC*

☐ Excellent   ☐ Very Good   ☐ Good
☐ Fair   ☐ Below Average   ☐ Poor

What did you like MOST about this book? _____
_____

What did you like LEAST about this book? _____
_____

How did you use this book (problem-solver, tutorial, reference...)?
_____

What is your level of computer expertise?
☐ New   ☐ Dabbler   ☐ Hacker
☐ Power User   ☐ Programmer   ☐ Experienced Professional

How did you find the pace of this book? _____

Please describe any problems you may have encountered with installing or using the utilities: _____
_____
_____

What computer languages are you familiar with? _____
_____

Please describe your computer hardware:

Computer _____ Hard disk _____
5.25" disk drives_____ 3.5" disk drives _____
Video card _____ Monitor _____
Printer _____ Peripherals _____
Sound Board _____ CD ROM _____

Where did you buy this book?
☐ Bookstore (name): _____
☐ Discount store (name): _____
☐ Computer store (name): _____
☐ Catalog (name): _____
☐ Direct from WGP   ☐ Other _____

What price did you pay for this book? _____

What influenced your purchase of this book?
☐ Recommendation   ☐ Advertisement
☐ Magazine review   ☐ Store display
☐ Mailing   ☐ Book's format
☐ Reputation of Waite Group Press   ☐ Other

How many computer books do you buy each year? _____

How many other Waite Group books do you own? _____

What is your favorite Waite Group book? _____
_____

Is there any program or subject you would like to see Waite Group Press cover in a similar approach? _____
_____

Additional comments? _____
_____
_____

☐ **Check here for a free Waite Group catalog**

Making Movies on Your PC

Waite Group Press
Attention: *Making Movies on Your PC*
200 Tamal Plaza
Corte Madera, CA 94925